Student Edition

Cadenza the Cat™, Bebop the Cat™, Gusto the Bulldog™, Largo the Snail™, P.F. (Piano Forte)™, Octavia™, and Maestro™
are trademarks of Warner Bros. Publications. All Rights Reserved.

Expressions Music Curriculum™, Music Expressions™, Band Expressions™, Jazz Expressions™,
Orchestra Expressions™, Choral Expressions™, Piano Expressions™, and Guitar Expressions™
are trademarks of Warner Bros. Publications. All Rights Reserved.

1 2 3 4 5 6 7 8 9 10   08 07 06 05 04 03

© 2003 WARNER BROS. PUBLICATIONS U.S. INC.
All Rights Reserved

Warner Bros. Publications • 15800 NW 48th Avenue • Miami, FL 33014

COMPLETE TEACHER EDITION (EMC5001)
UPC: 6-54979-06130-0
ISBN: 0-7579-1403-9 90000

TEACHER EDITION, VOLUME I (EMC5001A)
UPC: 6-54979-06311-7
ISBN: 0-7579-1404-7 90000

TEACHER EDITION, VOLUME II (EMC5001B)
UPC: 6-54979-06312-4
ISBN: 0-7579-1405-5 90000

TEACHER EDITION, VOLUME III (EMC5001C)
UPC: 6-54979-06313-1
ISBN: 0-7579-1406-3 90000

TEACHER EDITION, VOLUME IV (EMC5001D)
UPC: 6-54979-06314-8
ISBN: 0-7579-1407-1 90000

STUDENT EDITION (EMC5002)
UPC: 6-54979-06315-5
ISBN: 0-7579-1408-X 90000

Credits

PROJECT CREATORS & COORDINATORS

Robert W. Smith

Susan L. Smith

PROJECT EDITOR

Judith M. Stoehr

AUTHORS

Judith M. Stoehr
Lead Author
Creative Insights
Omaha, Nebraska

June M. Hinckley
Department of Education
Tallahassee, Florida

Darla S. Hanley, Ph.D.
Shenandoah University
Winchester, Virginia

Carolyn C. Minear
Orange County Public Schools
Orlando, Florida

CONTRIBUTING AUTHORS

Timothy S. Brophy, Ph.D.
Assessment Specialist
University of Florida
Gainesville, Florida

Art Williams
Media Specialist
Troy, Alabama

CONSULTANTS

June M. Hinckley
National Standards for the Arts
Consultant
Department of Education
Tallahassee, Florida

James Clarke
Fine Art Consultant
Executive Director
Texas Coalition for Quality Arts
Education
Houston, Texas

Kathy Robinson
Multicultural Consultant
Eastman School of Music
Rochester, New York

David Peters
Technology Coordinator
University of Indiana
Indianapolis, Indiana

Doug Brasell
Website Coordinator
Cairo, Georgia

Artie Almeida
Listening Maps
Bear Lake Elementary School
Apopka, Florida

MULTICULTURAL AMBASSADORS & CONTRIBUTORS

Toshio Akayama
Professor Emerita
Musashino School of Music
Tokyo, Japan

Gloria Kiester
Professor Emerita
St. Olaf College
Northfield, Minnesota

Kathy Robinson
Eastman School of Music
Rochester, New York

ORCHESTRA

Kathleen DeBerry Brungard
Charlotte, North Carolina

Gerald E. Anderson
Los Angeles, California

Michael L. Alexander
Houston, Texas

Sandra Dackow
Trenton, New Jersey

Anne C. Witt
Arlington, Texas

BAND

Jim Campbell
Lexington, Kentucky

Richard C. Crain
The Woodlands, Texas

Linda Gammon
Fairfax, Virginia

Gary Markham
Atlanta, Georgia

Michael Story
Houston, Texas

JAZZ

J. Richard Dunscomb
Atlanta, Georgia

Jose Diaz
Houston, Texas

Dr. Willie L. Hill, Jr.
Amherst, Massachusetts

Jerry Tolson
Louisville, Kentucky

CHORAL

Dr. Russell L. Robinson
Gainesville, Florida

Jim Kimmel
Franklin, Tennessee

Stan McGill
Garland, Texas

Josephine Lee
Chicago, Illinois

CONTRIBUTORS
Pilot and Practicing Teachers:

Kara Bell, *Great Falls, MT*

Cheryl Black, *Camden, SC*

W. Elaine Blocher, *Derby, KS*

Karen Bouton, *Graceville, FL*

Patty Brennan, *Chesapeake, VA*

Temetia Creed, *Tampa, FL*

Scott T. Evans, *Orlando, FL*

Debbie Fahmie, *Kissimmee, FL*

David Fox, *Oviedo, FL*

Mary Gibson, *Maitland, FL*

Claudette Gray, *Pittsburgh, PA*

Lisa Hamer, *Moncks Corner, SC*

Julie Harmon, *North Platte, NE*

Jennifer Hartman, *Shawnee, KS*

Elaine Hashem, *Penacook, NH*

Mark Hodges, *Sumter, SC*

Beverly Holl, *Los Angeles, CA*

Grace Jordan, *Orlando, FL*

Lyn Koch, *Pittsburgh, PA*

Eunice Marrero, *Orlando, FL*

Nancy McBride, *Anderson, SC*

Kathleen Scott Meske,
Los Angeles, CA

Deborah Mosier, *Bennington, NE*

Debi Noel, *Eugene, OR*

Keisha C. Pendergrass,
Clover, SC

Teresa Sims, *Troy, AL*

Marjorie Smith, *Lutz, FL*

Lisa Stern, *Winter Park, FL*

Julie A. Swank, *Troy, OH*

Jane Wall, *Wexford, PA*

Kirsten H. Wilcox,
Winchester, VA

Leslie A. Wooten, *LaGrange, KY*

RECORDING

Robert Dingley
Executive Producer

Robert W. Smith
Producer

Jack Lamb
Associate Producer

Kendall Thomsen
Recording Engineer

Andy de Ganahl
Mix Engineer

Jason May
Mix Engineer

MUSIC ARRANGING

Robert W. Smith

Michael Story

Jack Bullock

Victor Lopez

Timothy S. Brophy

Bill Galliford
Piano Accompaniments

Tod Edmondson
Piano Accompaniments

Ethan Neuburg
Piano Accompaniments

Kevin MacKelvie
Piano Accompaniments

WARNER BROS. PUBLICATIONS

Fred Anton
CEO

Robert Dingley
Vice President: Education

David Hakim
Vice President: Sales

Andrea Nelson
Vice President: Marketing

Lourdes Carreras-Balepogi
Marketing Coordinator

David Olsen
Director: Business Affairs

PRODUCTION

Judith M. Stoehr
Project Manager

Thom Proctor
Production Manager

Gayle Giese
Production Editor

Bill Galliford
Music Arranging Assistance

Donna Wheeler
Editorial Assistance

Heather Mahone
Editorial Assistance

Susan Buckey
Editorial Assistance

Arlene Sukraw, Ed.D.
Editorial Assistance

Nadine DeMarco
Text Proofreader

Nancy Rehm
Senior Art Director

Shawn Martinez
Assisant Art Director

Credits

Al Nigro
Music Engraving Manager

Mark Young
Music Engraver

Glenda Mikell
Music Engraver

Glyn Dryhurst
Director, Production Services

Hank Fields
Production Coordinator

Sharon Marlow
Production Assistance

**TEACHER EDITION
INTERIOR LAYOUT**

InterMedia
A Mad 4 Marketing Company

Margaret Stapleton
Project Director

Anne Rogers
Production Coordinator

Marie LaFauci
Senior Artist

Maureen Hyman

Leo Jones

Dana Kaufman

Roque Rodón

Linda Smith

Elyse Taylor

Amy Wertzler

Michelle M. White

**ACKNOWLEDGMENTS
Thanks to:**

Barbara Zimmerman, President: BZ/Rights & Permissions, Inc., for the work in securing the rights and permissions for the fine art and photography.

Donald Norsworthy, for photography of Mr. Art and Music Expressions™ characters.

Steve Palm, Vice President, Scholastic Marketing Partners, Scholastic Inc., for marketing consultation.

Gino Silva, Art Director, Scholastic Marketing Partners, Scholastic Inc., for cover and logo designs.

West Music, for use of instrument photos.

Linda Tracy, for the information on "The Versatile Piano" on Student Book pages 126–127.

Oxford University Press, for the information on Morris dances on Teacher Edition pages 47–48. Used by permission.

Priddis Music, Inc., for the accompaniment track for "Rock Around the Clock" (CD 9, Track 4).

Dennis Keeley, for the photo of Take 6 on Student Book pages 224–225.

Dwight Carter, for the photo of Sweet Honey in the Rock on Student Book pages 104–105.

Nicole Greggs, music teacher, and Plantation Park Elementary School, Plantation, Florida, for the use of their instruments for photographs.

William Claxton for the photo of Randy Newman on Student Book pages 160–161.

Student page 213:
SAN FRANCISCO
(Be Sure to Wear Some Flowers in Your Hair)
Words and Music by
John Phillips
© 1967, 1970 Universal-MCA Music Publishing,
A Division of Universal Studios, Inc.
Copyright Renewed
All Rights Reserved

Student page 213:
OHIO
Words and Music by
Neil Young
© 1970 Broken Arrow Music Corporation
Copyright Renewed
All Rights Reserved

Nicole Pouliot at Impact Artist Management, for the photo of Angélique Kidjo on Student Book page 92.

ILLUSTRATION CREDITS
(Student Edition page/Teacher Edition page)

1/4. Martha Ramirez
2–3/5. Judit Martinez
4–5/6. Martha Ramirez
6–7/7. Martha Ramirez
10–13/16. Janel Harrison
14–15/17. Ernesto Ebanks
16–17/18. Thais Yanes
18–19/18. Thais Yanes
20–23/25. Thais Yanes
22–23/25. Thais Yanes
24–25/26. Thais Yanes
26–27/34. Thais Yanes
28–29/35. Thais Yanes
30–31/37. Lisa Greene Mane
32–33/37. Lisa Greene Mane
34–35/38. Robert Ramsay
40–41/45. Robert Ramsay
42–43/46. Robert Ramsay
44–45/49. Lisa Greene Mane
46–47/56. Jeannette Aquino
48–51/58. Jeannette Aquino
52–53/59. Ken Rehm
56–57/65. Ernesto Ebanks
58–59/66. Jeannette Aquino
60–61/68. Jeannette Aquino
62–63/69. Lisa Greene Mane
66–67/77. Ken Rehm
68–71/80. Jeannette Aquino
72–73/84. Lisa Greene Mane
74–75/91. Robert Ramsay
76–77/92. Cardan Tuc Escobar
78–79/94. Lisa Greene Mane
80–81/98. Candy Woolley
82–83/99. Candy Woolley
84–85/100. Robert Ramsay
86–89/106. Thais Yanes
90–91/107. Robert Ramsay
94–95/115. Cardan Tuc Escobar
96–97/116. Jeannette Aquino
98–99/118. Candy Woolley
102–103/122. Martha Ramirez
106–107/126. Martha Ramirez
108–109/127. Martha Ramirez
110–111/129. Martha Ramirez
112–113/136. Cardan Tuc Escobar
114–115/137. Lisa Greene Mane
116/139. Lisa Greene Mane
117/166. Lisa Greene Mane
118–119/167. Jeannette Aquino
120–121/169. Lisa Greene Mane
124–125/171. Martha Ramirez
126–127/168. Lisa Greene Mane
130–131/179. Joe Klucar
132–133/179. Candy Woolley
134–135/181. Judit Martinez
136–137/183. Candy Woolley
138–139/189. Lisa Greene Mane
144–145/191. Janel Harrison
146–147/198. Thais Yanes
150–151/199. Martha Ramirez
152–157/200–201. Martha Ramirez
158–159/207. Thais Yanes
162–163/208. Jeannette Aquino
164–165/214. Nancy Rehm
166–167/216. Martha Ramirez
168–169/223. Candy Woolley
170–171/225. Judit Martinez
172–173/228. Jeannette Aquino
176–177/232. Candy Woolley
178–179/232–233. Candy Woolley
182–183/245. Ken Rehm
184–189/246–247. Judit Martinez
192–193/253. Robert Ramsay
194–195/254. Martha Ramirez
196–197/258. Ken Rehm
198–199/259. Lisa Greene Mane
202–203/261. Lisa Greene Mane
208–209/264. Martha Ramirez
212–213/269. Lisa Greene Mane
218–221/273. Robert Ramsay
222–223/278–279. Lisa Greene Mane
226–227/281. Nancy Rehm
228–229/282. Nancy Rehm
230–231/283. Lisa Greene Mane
232–233/290. Judit Martinez

Credits

Fine Art Credits

Two Over Three, by Tom Berg. Oil on canvas. 30 x 40 in. © 2001 Tom Berg.
   pg. 8 Student Edition   pg. 8 Teacher Edition

The Ripon City Morris Dancers taken by Graham Lindley © 1995. Used by permission of Ross-Parry Picture Agency.
   pg. 36 Student Edition   pg. 39 Teacher Edition

A double flageolet, a German flute, a bass recorder, a double flageolet, and a recorder from "Musical Instruments," by Alfred James Hipkins (1826–1903) (litho). Stapleton Collection, UK/Bridgeman Art Library.
   pg. 38 Student Edition   pg. 45 Teacher Edition

Popoyan (Columbian) Pectoral, 1100–1500 AD. Cast gold-copper alloy, gilded. Height 11¾ in. © The British Museum.
   pg. 54 Student Edition   pg. 60 Teacher Edition

Drum (ntan drum), Osei Bonsu, 1900–1977, Asante peoples, Ghana, ca. 1935. Wood, hide, paint, metal. H x W x D: 102.9 x 38.1 x 48.9 cm (40½ x 15 x 19¼ in). Gift of Dr. Robert Portman 81-20-1. Transparency: Photograph by Franko Khoury. National Museum of African Art, Smithsonian Institution.
   pg. 100 Student Edition   pg. 118 Teacher Edition

Square Piano, 19th century CE, by Francisco Florez. ca. 1800. Transparency: © Victoria & Albert Museum, London/Art Resource, NY.
   pg. 128 Student Edition   pg. 173 Teacher Edition

Harpsichord, London, 1743, from the Hugo Worch Collection. Transparency: Aldo Tutino/Art Resource, NY.
   pg. 129 Student Edition   pg. 173 Teacher Edition

Rouen Cathedral at Sunset, 1894, by Claude Monet (1840–1926). Transparency: Pushkin Museum, Russia/Bridgeman Art Library.
   pg. 142 Student Edition   pg. 191 Teacher Edition

Harpsichord, 17th Century CE, French. 1681. Japanned black and red with chinoiserie decoration in gold and silver. Inscribed by Jean-Antoine Vaudrt, instrument maker to Louis XIV. Transparency: © Victoria & Albert Museum, London/Art Resource, NY.
   pg. 148 Student Edition   pg. 199 Teacher Edition

Jaws, by Gil Mayers. 1991. Private collection/Gil Mayers/SuperStock.
   pg. 148 Student Edition   pg. 199 Teacher Edition

Two Girls at the Piano by Auguste Renoir (1841–1919). Oil on canvas. 112 x 79 cm. Transparency: © Réunion des Musées Nationaux/Art Resource, NY. Photo: J. G. Berizzi.
   pg. 148 Student Edition   pg. 199 Teacher Edition

Five Hat Forms, 2000, by Kathi Packer. Oil on linen. 26 x 52 in. © Kathi Packer.
   pg. 174 Student Edition   pg. 231 Teacher Edition

A Sunday on La Grande Jatte—1884, 1884–86 by Georges Seurat (1859–1891). Oil on canvas, 207.6 x 308 cm. Helen Birch Bartlett Memorial Collection, 1926.22.
   pg. 214 Student Edition   pg. 270 Teacher Edition

Park Near Lucerne, 1938 by Paul Klee. Oil and color paste on paper, mounted on jute burlap. 40 x 28 in. © 2003 Artists Rights Society (ARS), New York/VG Bild-Kunst, Bonn. Transparency: Paul-Klee-Stiftung, Kunstmuseum Bern, Inv. No. B 27.
   pg. 215 Student Edition   pg. 270 Teacher Edition

Contents

Contents

Maestro

Lift Every Voice and Sing

By JAMES WELDON JOHNSON
and J. ROSAMOND JOHNSON
Arranged by ROBERT W. SMITH

Lift ev-'ry voice and sing, till earth and heav - en ring, ring with the har - mo - nies of lib - er - ty. Let our re - joic - ing rise high as the lis - t'ning skies, let it re - sound loud as the roll - ing sea.

Sing a song full of the faith that the

dark past has taught us. Sing a

song full of the hope that the pres - ent has

brought_____ us. Fac - ing the ris -

ing sun of our new day

be - gun, let us march on till vic - to -

ry_____ is won._____

6

Twos and Threes

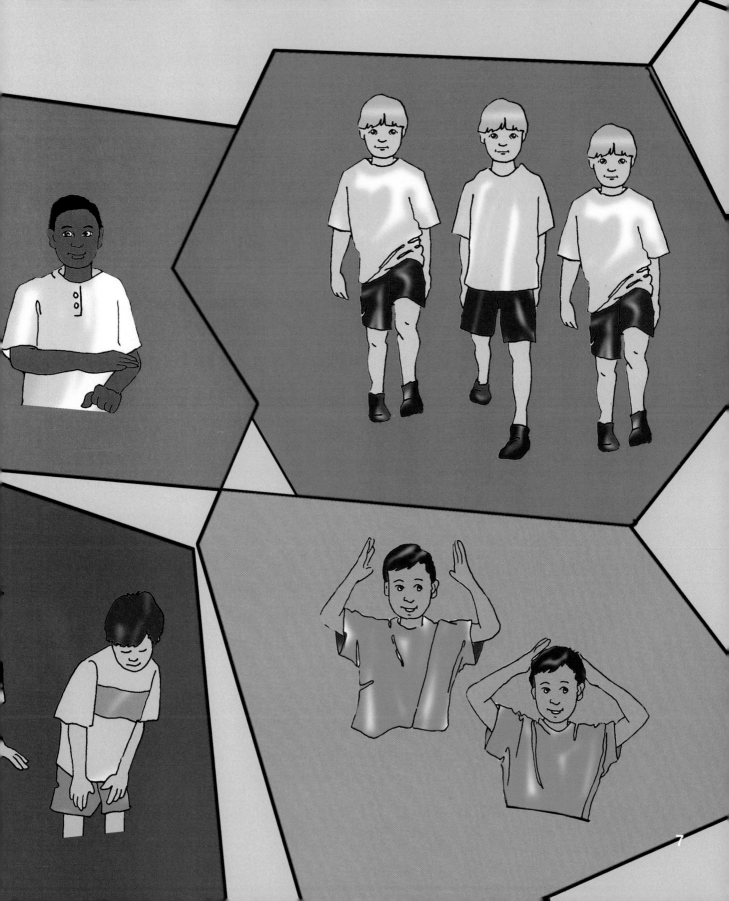

Two Over Three by Tom Berg

- **Why do you think the artist called this painting "Two Over Three"?**

- **What type of meter could the chairs represent in music?**

- **What type of meter could the balls represent in music?**

Put a Little Love in Your Heart

By JIMMY HOLIDAY, RANDY MYERS
and JACKIE DE SHANNON
Arranged by ROBERT W. SMITH

Think of your fel - low man, lend him a help - ing hand,

put a lit-tle love___ in your heart.___

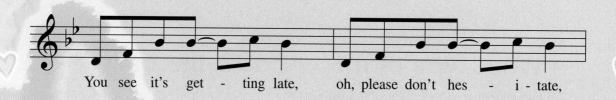

You see it's get - ting late, oh, please don't hes - i - tate,

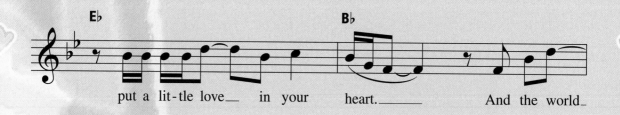

put a lit-tle love___ in your heart.___ And the world___

___ will be a bet - ter place, and the world___

___ will be a bet - ter place for

you   and me.   You just wait___   and

F7   B♭

see.   Think of your fel - low man, lend him a   help - ing hand,

E♭   B♭
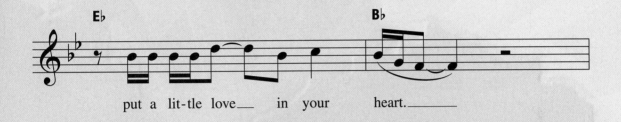
put a lit-tle love___ in your   heart.___

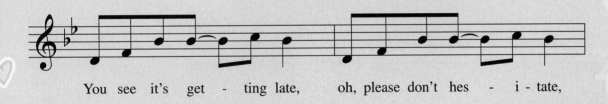
You see it's get - ting late,   oh, please don't hes - i - tate,

E♭   B♭
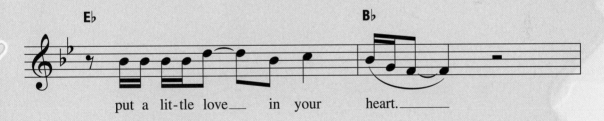
put a lit-tle love___ in your   heart.___

B♭
Interlude

And the world___   will be a

Cm   F   B♭   Cm   F

bet-ter place, and the world___   will be a bet-ter place   for

you   and me.   You just wait___   and see.

Think of your fel - low man,   lend him a   help - ing hand,

put a lit-tle love___   in your   heart._____

You see it's get - ting late,   oh, please don't hes - i - tate,

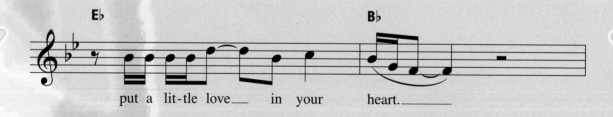

put a lit-tle love___   in your   heart._____

Put a lit-tle love,___ put a lit-tle love,   put a lit-tle love,___ put a lit-tle love,

put a lit-tle love___   in your   heart._____

notation

The written notes and symbols that are used to represent music

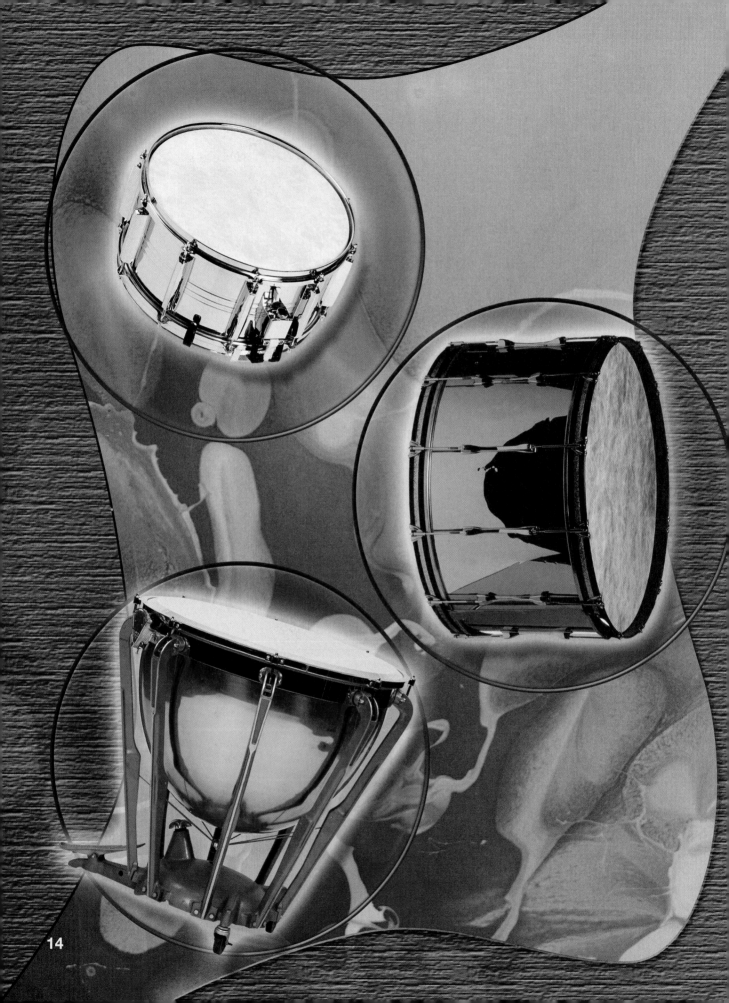

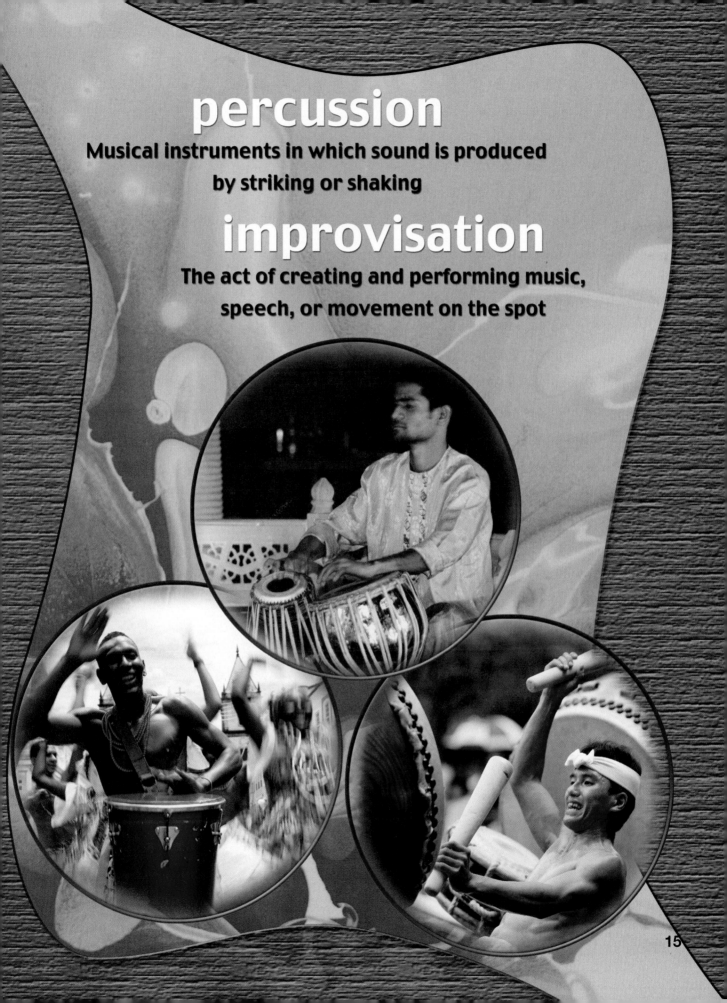

percussion
Musical instruments in which sound is produced by striking or shaking

improvisation
The act of creating and performing music, speech, or movement on the spot

We Are the World

The song "We Are the World" was written and performed as part of the Food for Africa project, headed up by Michael Jackson, Lionel Richie, and Tina Turner. The organizers' goal was to help stamp out hunger in Africa. Proceeds from the sales of the recordings went to the U.S.A. for Africa fund. "We Are the World" was written by Michael Jackson and Lionel Richie and produced by Quincy Jones. Singers such as Kenny Rogers, Michael Jackson, Paul Simon, Diana Ross, Kenny Loggins, Bette Midler, Al Jarreau, Harry Belafonte, Stevie Wonder, Lionel Richie, Cyndie Lauper, Tina Turner, Ray Charles, Bruce Springsteen, and many others performed together for the recording. The recording won several awards, including Grammys for Best Pop Performance by a Duo or Group With Vocal, Song of the Year, Record of the Year, and Best Music Video, Short Form.

he World

Lean on Me

By BILL WITHERS
Arranged by ROBERT W. SMITH

Some - times in our lives____ we all have pain,____

____ we all have sor - row.____

But if we are wise,____ we know that there's____

____ al - ways to - mor - row.____ Lean on me____

____ when you're not strong,_ I'll be your friend,_

____ I'll help you car - ry on,____

for it won't be long____ 'til I'm gon - na need_

Composers use lyrics to tell a story or express an idea.

lyrics
Words of a song

personal repertoire
A collection of songs you know and can sing or play

Make a list in your journal of five songs you know and can sing.

Lean on Me

Verse:

By BILL WITHERS
Arranged by ROBERT W. SMITH

Vocal and Recorder

Some - times in our lives_ we all have pain,_ we all have sor - row._ But if we are wise,_ we know that there's_ al - ways to - mor - row._ Lean on me_ when you're not strong,_ I'll be your friend,_ I'll help you car - ry on,__ for it won't be long____ 'til I'm gon - na need_ some - bod - y to lean__ on._

major scale

A scale with half steps between the third and fourth and the seventh and eighth tones

interval

The distance between two pitches

half step

The smallest interval between two notes

whole step

A musical interval equal to two half steps

The key signature at the beginning of a song tells us where to find "do," which is home base for a major scale. "Lean on Me" has one sharp—F—and is in the key of G major.

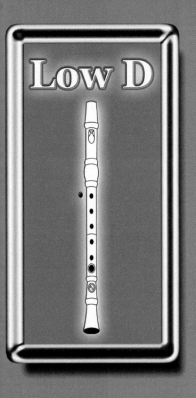

Low D

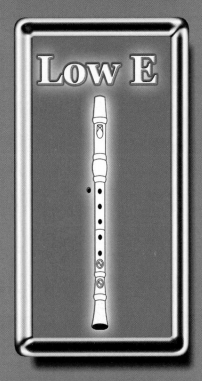

Low E

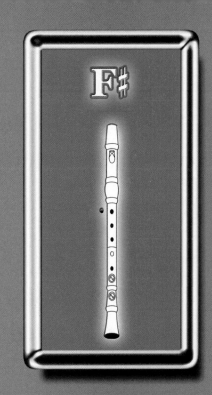

F#

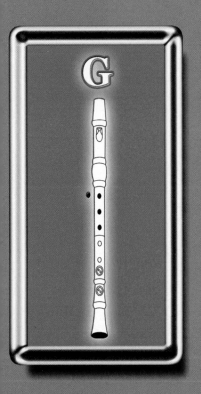

G

recorder

A woodwind instrument with fingerholes played by blowing through a mouthpiece at the top

treble clef

The clef for higher vocal and instrumental parts

key signature

The group of sharps or flats placed to the right of the clef on a musical staff to identify the key

sharp

A symbol that raises the pitch of a note one half step

flat

A symbol that lowers the pitch of a note one half step

accidental

A flat or sharp that is written in the music instead of the key signature

Sing Me a Song

Words and Music by
LEONARD ENNS
Arranged by MICHAEL STORY

pitched

Musical instruments that are able to make a specific musical tone

unpitched

Musical instruments that are unable to make a specific musical tone

percussion family

A group of instruments that are sounded by shaking or by striking one object with another

BASS DRUM

SNARE DRUM

TIMPANI

The Ripon City Morris Dancers

- What do you notice about the dancers' costumes?

- What do you suppose is on their hats? Why?

- To what kind of music do you think they are performing? How can you tell?

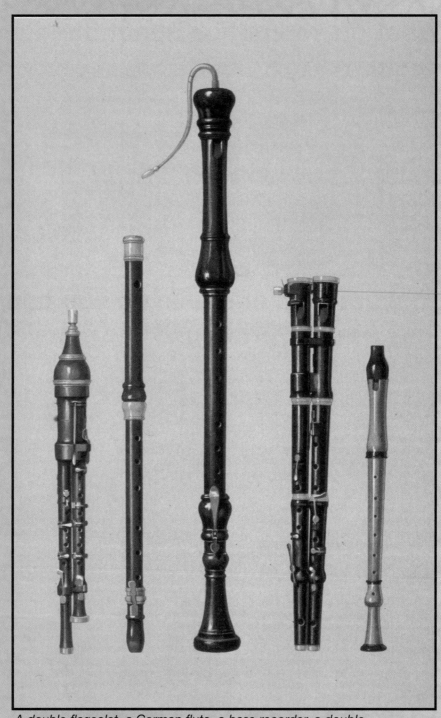

A double flageolet, a German flute, a bass recorder, a double flageolet, and a recorder from "Musical Instruments" by Alfred James Hipkins

- **This artwork contains a double flageolet, a German flute, a bass recorder, a double flageolet, and a recorder.**

- **Which instrument do you think is the German flute? Why?**

- **Which instrument is the bass recorder? How do you know?**

- **Which instruments are different from each other? How are they different?**

BEAN SETTING

TRADITIONAL ENGLISH DANCE
Arranged by PAUL KERLEE

o = dib
x = stick tap

BEAN SETTING

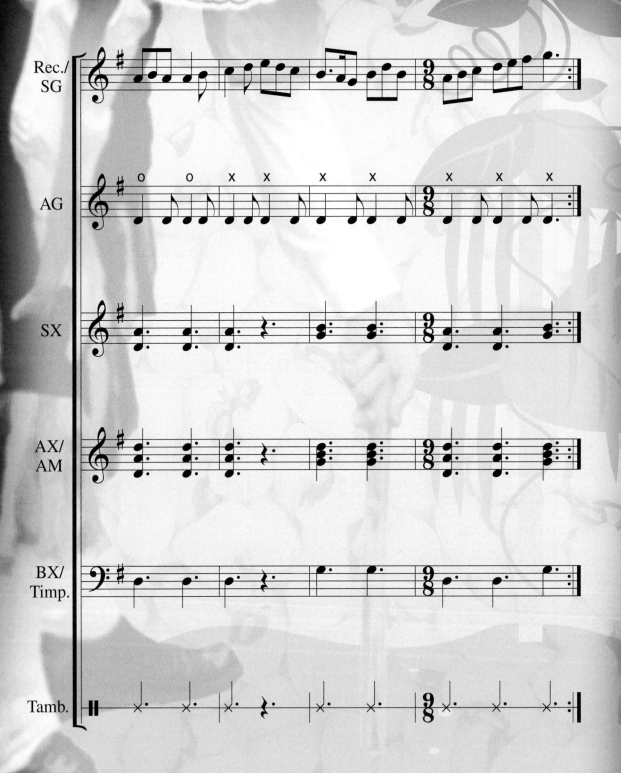

score
The written form of a musical composition

time signature

The symbol usually at the beginning of the staff that indicates the meter

jingle bells

castanets

guiro

triangle

tambourine

woodblock

claves

cymbals

whip

auxiliary percussion

Percussion instruments that add color or contrast in an orchestra or band

43

chord
**Three or more tones
sounded at the same time**

arpeggio
**The notes of a chord
sounded one after the other**

octave

A tone that is eight full tones above or below another given tone that shares the same name

introduction

A section of music at the beginning of a composition

45

Tender Shepherd

from *Peter Pan*

Music by MARK CHARLAP
Lyrics by CAROLYN LEIGH
Arranged by MICHAEL STORY

① Sing in unison or canon

legato

F **Gm** **Am** **Gm**

mp Ten - der shep - herd, ten - der shep - herd,

② **F** **Gm** **Am** **Gm**

let me help you count your sheep.

③ **F** **Gm** **Am** **Gm**

One in the mead - ow, two in the gar - den,

Repeat as needed for canon

F **Gm** **Am** **Gm**

three in the nurs - er - y fast a - sleep.

legato – Smooth and connected

mezzo piano – Medium soft

piano – Soft

J. Aquino

ALE BRIDER

minor scale
A scale with half steps between the second and third and the fifth and sixth tones

relative minor
The scale that begins on the sixth tone or "la" of the major scale with the same key signature

J. AQUINO

ALE BRIDER

TRADITIONAL JEWISH SONG
Arranged by JACK BULLOCK

Some are broke and some are wealth - y,
oy yoy, some are wealth - y, some are sick and
some are health - y, oy yoy yoy.
Some can sing, but oth - ers can't sing, oy yoy,
oth - ers can't sing. All are lov - ing, laugh - ing, danc - ing,
oy yoy yoy! Oy yoy yoy yoy yoy yoy
oy yoy yoy yoy yoy yoy oy yoy yoy
yoy yoy yoy yoy yoy yoy yoy.
yoy yoy yoy yoy yoy.

Consonant

solo

A performance by one person, with or without accompaniment

duet

A performance by two people, with or without accompaniment

forte f

Loud

mezzo forte mf

Medium loud

Countdown

Menu

....	$22.95
P.	$24.95
D.	$25.95
S.	$28.95
CH.	$29.95
K.	$32.95
G.	$34.95
F.	$35.95
H.	$38.95
V.	$39.95
Z.	$42.95

Popoyan (Columbian) Pectoral, 1100–1500 AD

- In music duets, the parts must balance each other. In artwork, this balance is sometimes called symmetry.

- Do you see symmetry in the *Popoyan (Columbian) Pectoral*? Where?

- Is it made of wood or metal? How can you tell?

natural

Neither sharp nor flat

C

**New note
low C**

**New note
F**

F

57

CHICHIPAPA

TRADITIONAL JAPANESE SONG
Arranged by MICHAEL STORY

Voice and Recorder

Chi - chi - pa - pa, Chi - chi - pa

su - su me - no gak ko no sen - se - wa,

mu - chi - o fu - ri fu - ri chi - pa - pa

chi - chi - pa - pa chi - pa - pa.

© 2003 BEAM ME UP MUSIC (ASCAP)   All Rights Administered by WARNER BROS. PUBLICATIONS U.S. INC.   All Rights Reserved

ledger line

A short line placed above or below a staff to extend the lines and spaces

59

The Clocks
(in C)

TRADITIONAL DANISH ROUND
Arranged by MICHAEL STORY

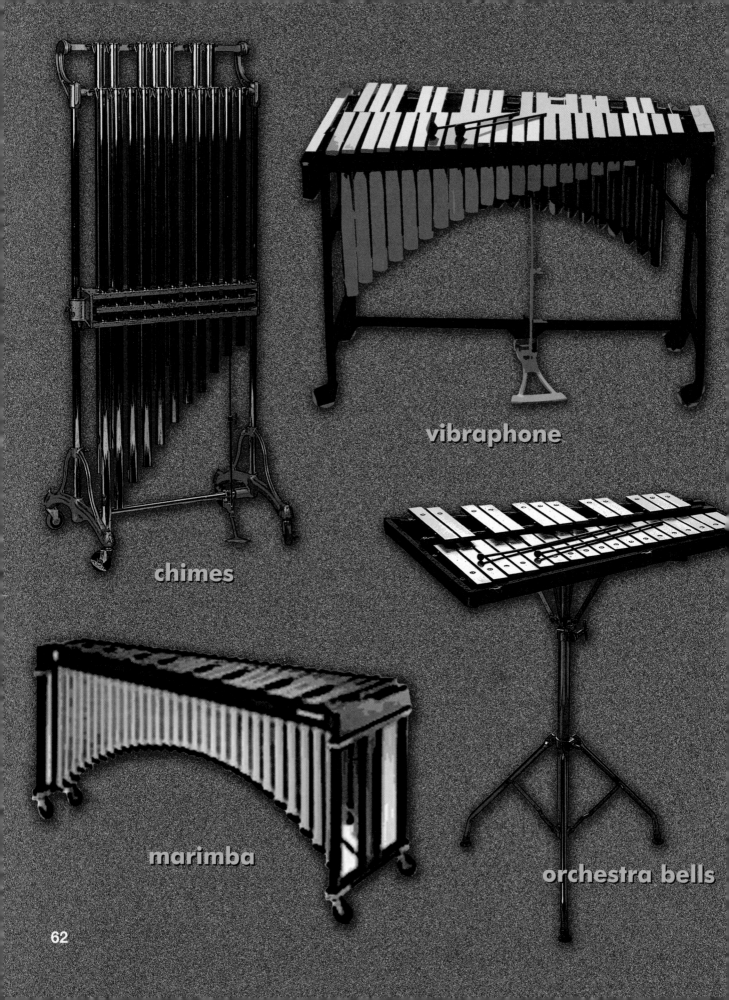

vibraphone

chimes

marimba

orchestra bells

62

percussionist

One who plays percussion instruments

ensemble

A group of musicians performing together

xylophone

Evelyn Glennie

Evelyn Glennie

(b. 1965)

Evelyn Glennie was born on a farm near Aberdeen, Scotland. She grew up there with her parents and two brothers. As a child, she studied piano and clarinet. From the ages of eight to 12, Evelyn lost most of her hearing from nerve damage. She fell in love with her favorite instrument, the snare drum. At the age of 19, Evelyn graduated from London's Royal Academy of Music with an honors degree. Evelyn plays barefoot. She hears her own instrument and the orchestra by feeling vibrations through the floor and in her own body. She plays conventional percussion instruments as well as ethnic instruments. She even plays such things as flowerpots and kitchen utensils. Evelyn Glennie is the world's only full-time percussion soloist.

The Mill Wheel

B♭

transpose

To write or perform music in a key other than the original or given key

countermelody

A second melody that is performed along with the main melody

The Mill Wheel

J'entends le Moulin

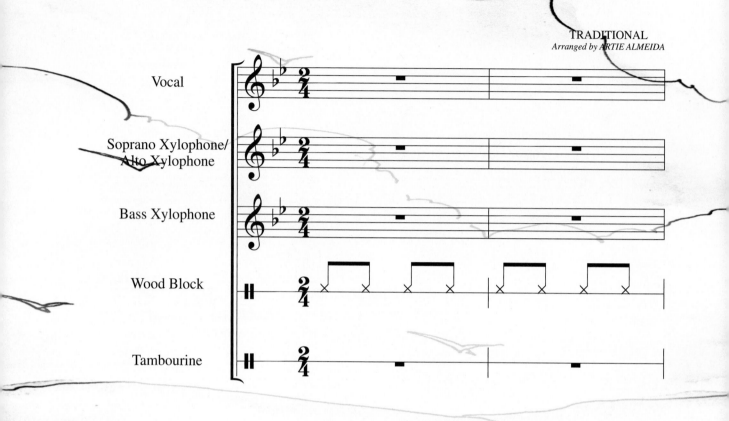

TRADITIONAL
Arranged by ARTIE ALMEIDA

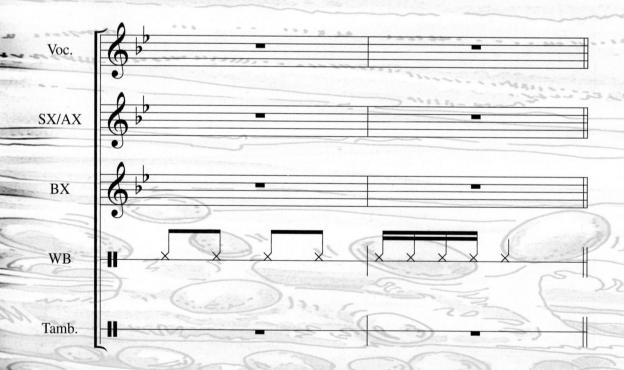

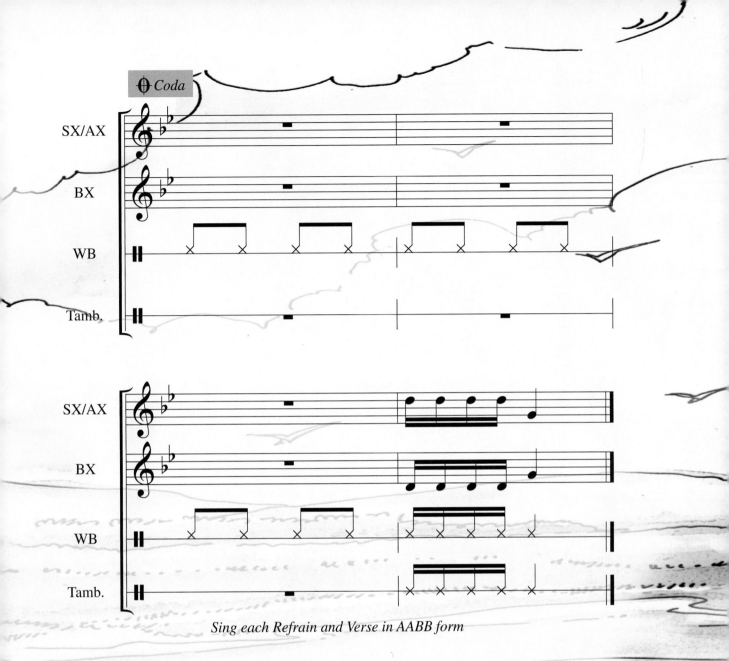

Sing each Refrain and Verse in AABB form

Refrain:
J'entends le moulin, tique tique taque;
I hear the mill-wheel, tick-a, tick-a, tack-a;
J'entends le moulin, taque;
I hear the mill-wheel, tack-a;
J'entends le moulin, tique tique taque;
I hear the mill-wheel, tick-a, tick-a, tack-a;
J'entends le moulin, taque.
I hear the mill-wheel, tack-a.

Verse 1:
Father is building us a house,
tique taque tique taque;
Carpenters three work on his house,
tique taque tique taque.

Refrain

Verse 2:
He who is the youngest of the three,
tique taque tique taque;
He is the dearest one to me,
tique taque tique taque.

Refrain

Verse 3:
"What do you bring as you pass by?"
tique taque tique taque;
"It's a tasty pigeon pie,"
tique taque tique taque.

Refrain

music criteria
Standards by which music can be evaluated

dress rehearsal
The final rehearsal before performing for an audience

steel drums
Mallet percussion instruments made from oil drums or barrels
whose tops have been hammered to create various pitches

Water Come to Me Eye

JAMAICAN FOLK SONG
Arranged by ROBERT W. SMITH

Ev - 'ry time I'm a - way from Li - za,

wa - ter come_ to me eye._ When I think_ a - bout

my gal Li - za, wa - ter come_ to me eye._

Come back, Li - za, come back, gal,_

wipe the tear_ from me eye._ Come back, Li - za,

come back, gal,_ wipe the tear_ from me eye._

Interlude

LINSTEAD MARKET

TRADITIONAL JAMAICAN SONG
Arranged by ROBERT W. SMITH

Calypso

Car - ry me ac - kee go a Lin - stead Mar - ket,

not a quat - ty worth sell. Car - ry me ac - kee go a

Lin - stead Mar - ket, not a quat - ty worth sell. Oh,

no! Not a mite, not a bite, what a Sat - ur - day

night! Oh, no! Not a mite, not a bite,

Interlude

what a Sat - ur - day night!

Car - ry me ac - kee go a Lin - stead Mar - ket,

not a quat - ty worth sell. Car - ry me ac - kee go a

Lin - stead Mar - ket, not a quat - ty worth sell. Oh,

no! Not a mite, not a bite, what a Sat - ur-day

night! Oh, no! Not a mite, not a bite,

what a Sat - ur-day night! What a Sat - ur-day night!

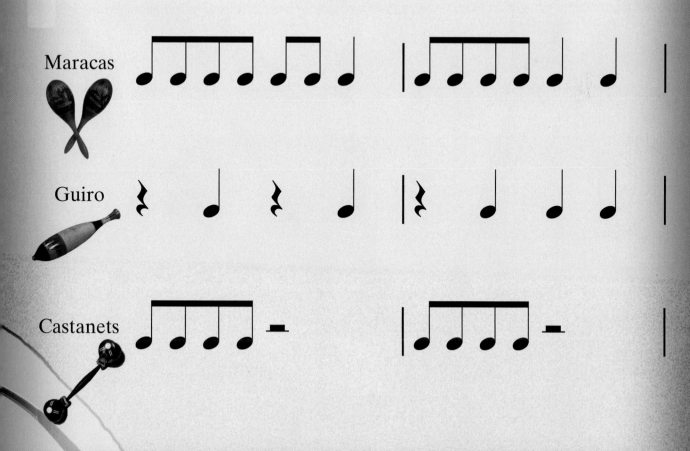

Maracas

Guiro

Castanets

Afghanistan

Pakistan

China

New Delhi

Nepal

Bangladesh

India

Hindu badregali festival

Man with tablas

Man with tambura

Woman playing sitar

Man playing sarod

India

India is a country in southern Asia that is the second largest country in the world in population. Only China has more people. India is also one of the most densely populated countries in the world and one of the largest in area. The capital of India is New Delhi. In addition to hot desert and tropical rain forests, India contains the world's largest mountain system—the Himalayas. The people of India are from many different ethnic groups and speak hundreds of languages. Hindi is the national language. Indian music dates back to ancient times. It sounds different from American and European music partly because it uses different scales and musical instruments. The notes of the Indian scale are arranged in various patterns called ragas. Each raga has a special meaning and may be associated with a mood, emotion, season, or time of day. Indian instruments include the sitar, sarod, and vina, which are plucked stringed instruments; the tambura, which produces a drone (continuous tone); and the tabla and mridangam, which are drums.

Carnaval musicians playing the pandeiro and cuicas

Drummers in street

Man beating drum

Men playing pandeiros

Boys playing drums

Brazil

Brazil is the largest country in South America—both in area and population. It occupies almost half the continent and has more people than all the other South American nations combined. Brazil contains the world's largest tropical rain forest and the mighty Amazon River. Brazil's people come from diverse backgrounds. About half the country's population are of European ancestry—mostly German, Italian, Portuguese, and Spanish. Many other Brazilians are of mixed African and European ancestry, and some are of only African descent. Indians, the original Brazilians, form less than one percent of Brazil's people. Music from Brazil gained attention in the 1900s when Antonio Carlos Jobim and João Gilberto composed songs in the bossa nova style. Sergio Mendes also wrote many tunes based on the Brazilian style. Brazilian instruments include the pandeiro, cuicas, surdo, agogo bells, and repinique.

Luiz Rio
2002

82

Venezuela

Guyana

Suriname

French Guiana

Colombia

ador

Peru

Brazil

Brasília

Bolivia

Chile

Paraguay

Argentina

Uruguay

ORDEM E PROGRESSO

LINSTEAD MARKET

Select Your Recorder Solo

When the Saints Go Marching In

Music by VIRGIL O. STAMPS
Lyrics by LUTHER G. PRESLEY

Theme From Beethoven's Ninth Symphony
(Ode to Joy)

LUDWIG VAN BEETHOVEN

86

Au Claire de la Lune

By JEAN-BAPTISTE LULLY

Swing Low, Sweet Chariot

AFRICAN-AMERICAN SPIRITUAL

Home on the Range

By DANIEL E. KELLY

Take Me Out to the Ball Game

Words by JACK NORWORTH
Music by ALBERT VON TILZER

Note Names:	Low C	Low D	Low E	F♮	F♯	G	A	B	C	D
Title:										
Ode to Joy		x				x	x	x	x	x
When the Saints Go Marching In		x	x		x	x	x			
Au Claire de la Lune						x	x	x		
Swing Low, Sweet Chariot		x	x			x	x	x		x
Home on the Range		x	x		x	x	x	x	x	x
Take Me Out to the Ball Game	x	x	x	x	x	x	x	x	x	x

Rhythmic Values:	♩	♫	𝅗𝅥	𝄽	𝅗𝅥.	♩. ♪	𝅝	𝅗𝅥.–♩	𝅝–♩	𝅗𝅥.–𝅗𝅥
Title:										
Ode to Joy	x	x	x			x				
When the Saints Go Marching In	x		x	x	x			x	x	
Au Claire de la Lune	x		x				x			
Swing Low, Sweet Chariot	x	x	x			x	x			
Home on the Range	x	x	x	x				x		x
Take Me Out to the Ball Game	x		x	x	x			x		

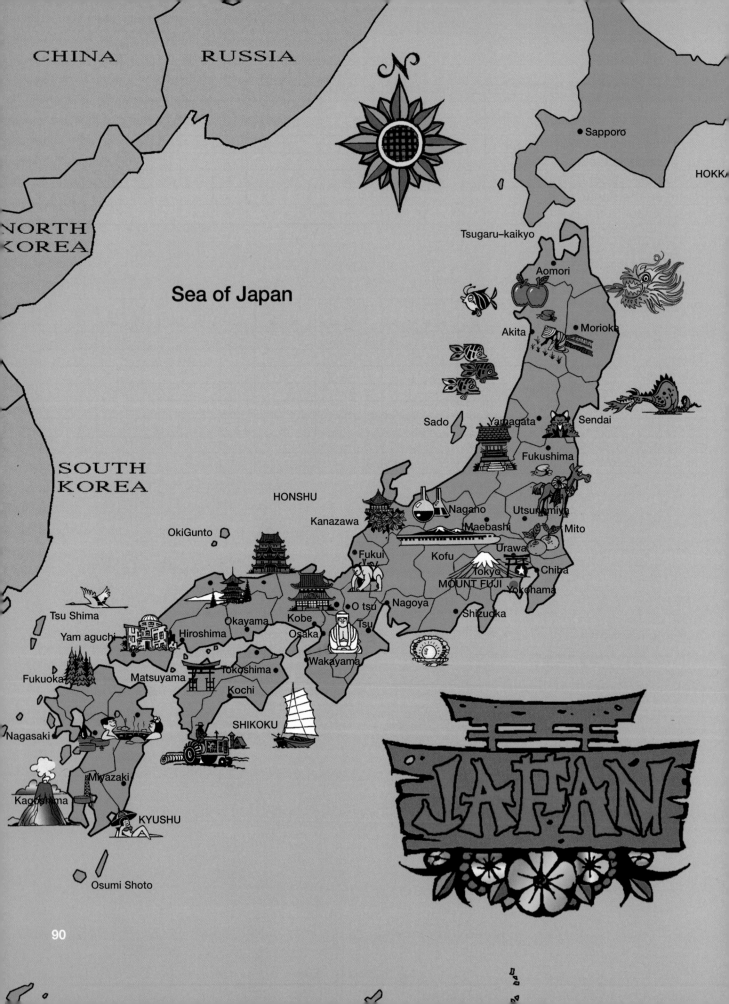

CHINA RUSSIA

N

HOKKA

NORTH
KOREA

Tsugaru–kaikyo

• Sapporo

Sea of Japan

Aomori

Akita

• Morioka

SOUTH
KOREA

Sado

Yamagata

Sendai

Fukushima

HONSHU

Kanazawa

Nagano

Utsunomiya

OkiGunto

Fukui

Maebashi

Mito

Kofu

MOUNT FUJI

Urawa

Tsu Shima

Okayama

O tsu

Nagoya

Tokyo

Chiba

Yam aguchi

Kobe

Tsu

Yokohama

Hiroshima

Osaka

Shizuoka

Fukuoka

Tokushima

Wakayama

Matsuyama

Nagasaki

Kochi

SHIKOKU

Miyazaki

KYUSHU

Kagoshima

Osumi Shoto

90

taiko

A large Japanese barrel-shaped drum played with two sticks

Angélique Kidjo

Angélique Kidjo

(b. 1960)

Angélique Kidjo was born July 14, 1960, in Benin, West Africa. Added to her African roots are Portuguese and English ancestries. Her recording *On Black Ivory Soul* explores the musical kinship between Africa and Brazil.

Angélique's solo career began in 1989, which meant going against society for both her and her supportive family. In Benin, women singers are considered to be inferior.

Angélique lives most of the time in Brooklyn, New York. She is a high-powered soprano in the pop culture. She performs tribal and pop rhythms of her West African heritage. She sings some numbers in English, French, and African languages Yoruba and Fon. She also blends a variety of styles, including funk, salsa, jazz, rumba, soul, and makossa.

Angélique says, "I believe music is the only way to heal pain and bring people together. It's a language beyond color of skin, country, or culture. I want to inspire people to think about poverty, freedom, and family on a deeper level."

SAHARA DESERT

TUNISIA

MOROCCO

ALGERIA

LIBYA

EGYPT

WESTERN SAHARA

MAURITANIA

MALI

NIGER

SUDAN

ERITREA

CAPE VERDE

SENEGAL

GAMBIA

GUINEA BISSAU

GUINEA

BURKINA FASO

BENIN

CHAD

DJIBOUTI

SOMALIA

SIERRA LEONE

IVORY COAST

GHANA

TOGO

NIGERIA

CAMEROON

CENTRAL AFRICAN REPUBLIC

ETHIOPIA

LIBERIA

EQUATORIAL GUINEA

SÃO TOMÉ & PRÍNCIPE

GABON

REPUBLIC OF THE CONGO

DEMOCRATIC REPUBLIC OF THE CONGO

KENYA

UGANDA

RWANDA

BURUNDI

TANZANIA

Indian Ocean

SEYCHEL

Atlantic Ocean

ZAMBIA

MALAWI

MOZAMBIQUE

COMOROS

ANGOLA

MADAGASCAR

NAMIBIA

ZIMBABWE

BOTSWANA

SWAZILAND

MAURITIUS

LESOTHO

SOUTH AFRICA

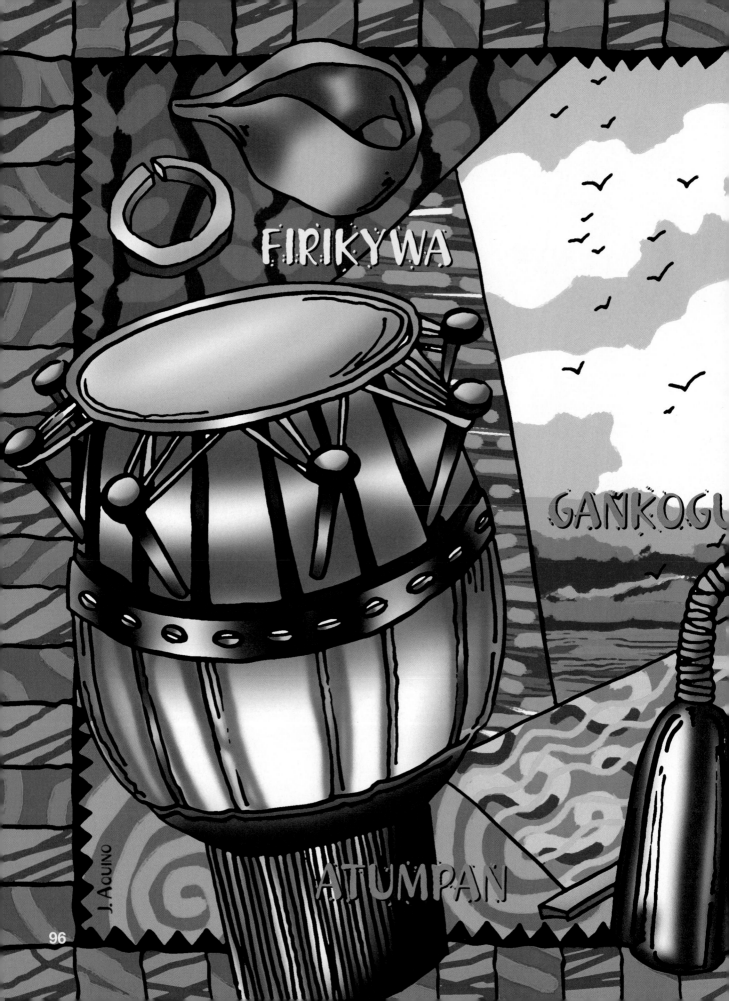

FIRIKYWA

GANKOGU

ATUMPAN

polyrhythms
Two or more rhythms
performed at the same time

ostinato
A repeated melodic
or rhythmic pattern

98

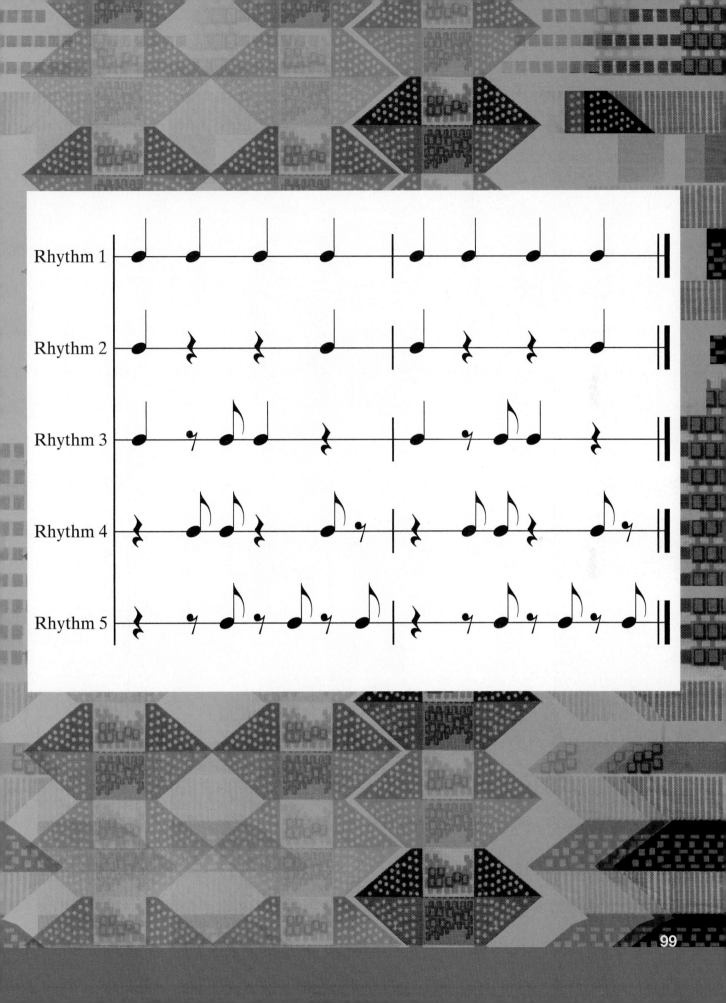

Drum (ntan drum), Osei Bonsu, Asante peoples, Ghana, Africa

- **What do you think is holding the drum in this artwork?**

- **What kind of sound would this drum make?**

- **How do you think the Asante people of Ghana would use this drum?**

Recorder Review

Low C
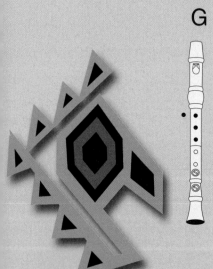

D

E

F

F#

G

A

B

C

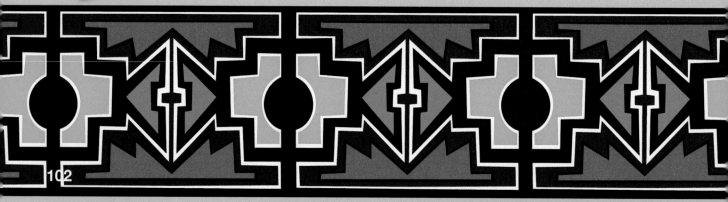

- Which of these notes does not belong in the C major scale? How do you know?

- What is an arpeggio?

- What are the letter names of the notes in the **I** chord in the key of C?

Left to right: Aisha Kahlil, Nitanju Bolade Casel, Bernice Johnson Reagon, Carol Maillard, Shirley Childress Saxton, and Ysaye Maria Barnwell

Sweet Honey in the Rock

Sweet Honey in the Rock is a Grammy® Award–winning a cappella ensemble of African-American women. Their first album was released in 1976. The name *Sweet Honey in the Rock* comes from a biblical parable that tells of a land so rich that when rocks were cracked open, honey flowed from them. The women in this group consider themselves to be as strong as a rock and as sweet as honey. Their music comes from deep roots in the sacred music of the black church—spirituals, hymns, and gospel—as well as jazz and blues. The artists compose, arrange, and perform songs with strong messages about the world they live in and the issues that concern them.

Allundé, Alluia

SWAHILI LULLABY
Arranged by ROBERT W. SMITH

2.

to Verses

Al - lun - dé, al - lu - ia.

lu - ia.   Al - lun - dé, al - lu - ia.

Verses

1. Je   pu   wah   yé   yé_____ ku - sah,
2. Man - dé   a - qua - qua a - qua - qua man - dé, }

Ai - yai - yai yé_____ al - lun - dé._____

Ai - yai - yai yé_____ ai - yai yé_____ al -

2nd time D.S. 𝄋 al Coda   Sing Verse 2

lun - dé._____

⊕ Coda

ritard.   mp   pp

Al - lun - dé, al - lu - ia._____

ritard.   mp   pp

lu - ia.   Al - lun - dé, al - lu - ia.

Dal Segno
Go back to the sign (*D.S.* 𝄋) and continue playing or singing from there

Dal Segno al Coda
Go back to the sign (*D.S.* 𝄋) and continue playing or singing from there until you see
To Coda ⊕. Then skip to the ⊕ *Coda* section and continue to the end.

first ending
First alternate ending to a repeated section

second ending
Second alternate ending to a repeated section

coda
A short ending section of music

pianissimo (*pp*)
Very soft

crescendo (<)
Gradually becoming louder

decrescendo (>)
Gradually becoming softer

tie
A curved line connecting two notes of the same pitch indicating they are to be played as one note

slur
A curved line connecting different notes on a staff to indicate they are to be performed smoothly

New Note C#

SHOSHOLOZA

TRADITIONAL SOUTH AFRICAN SONG
Arranged by MICHAEL STORY

grand staff
The bass clef and treble clef
staves together

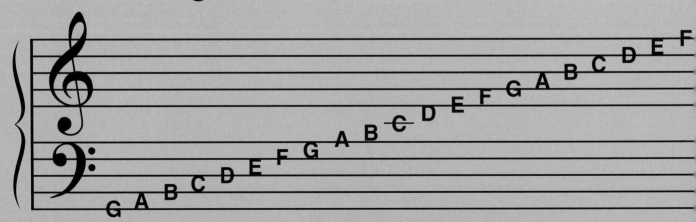

Why do you think the bass clef is sometimes called the F clef?

Intervals, steps, skips, repeated tones, and even chords are the same for the bass clef as for the treble clef. Only the note names are different.

bass clef
The clef for lower vocal and instrumental parts

harmony

Two or more musical tones
sounding at the same time

fourth

The interval from a given tone
to a fourth tone above or below it

fifth

The interval from a given tone
to a fifth tone above or below it

MAKE NEW FRIENDS

Canon

TRADITIONAL ENGLISH ROUND
Arranged by MICHAEL STORY

①

mf Make new friends, but keep the old,

②

③

one is sil - ver and the oth - er gold.

Make new friends, but keep the old,

Repeat as needed for canon

one is sil - ver and the oth - er gold.

I

canon

A musical form in which the same music is performed by two or more persons beginning at different times so they overlap

free canon

A musical form in which different versions of the same music are performed by two or more persons beginning at different times so they overlap

118

J. AQUINO

MAKE NEW FRIENDS

Free Canon

TRADITIONAL ENGLISH ROUND
Arranged by MICHAEL STORY

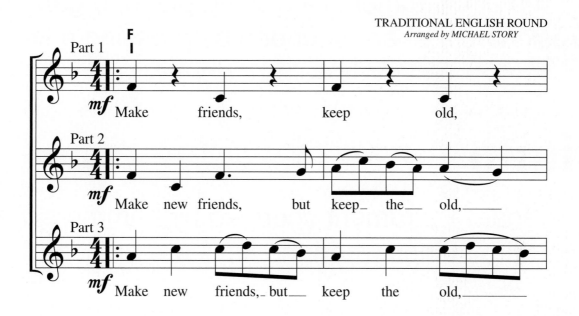

Repeat as needed for canon

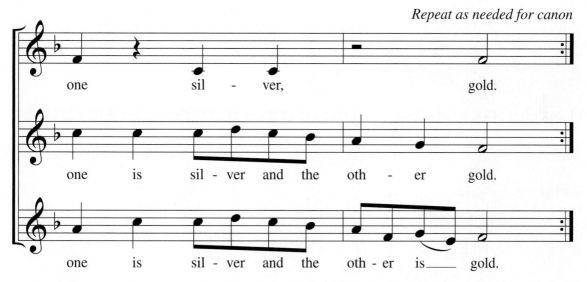

ornamentation
A note or group of notes that embellish or decorate the melody

119

keyboard family

A group of instruments including piano, organ, and harpsichord that are sounded by pressing a key

piano

A keyboard instrument sounded by hammers that strike wire strings when the keys are pressed

pipe organ

A musical instrument with one or more keyboards and sounded by pressing keys that send air through wood or metal pipes

harpsichord

A keyboard instrument sounded by strings that are plucked rather than struck

Canon in D
by Johann Pachelbel
1653–1706

Johann Pachelbel was a German organist and one of the greatest composers of the seventeenth century. Enjoy listening to one of his most revered pieces, "Canon in D." In this piece, "canon" means a repeating melody with variations.

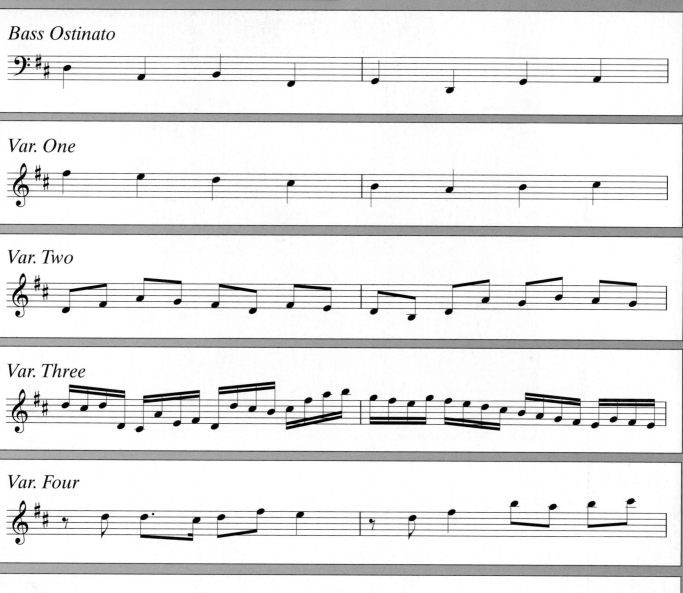

Bass Ostinato

Var. One

Var. Two

Var. Three

Var. Four

Var. Five

What did you observe about each part that entered?

Continue listening to the rest of the canon.
Notice how frequently both the texture and dynamics of the canon change.
Which part had the thickest texture? The thinnest? How did it end?
Which variation was your favorite?

121

Irving Berlin

Irving Berlin

(1888–1989)

Irving Berlin was born in Russia, but when he was a child, his parents immigrated to New York City. His first hit song was "Alexander's Ragtime Band." He is best known for writing "God Bless America," but he also wrote songs for many Broadway musicals and Hollywood movies. He lived to be over a hundred years old.

Ludwig van Beethoven

Ludwig van Beethoven

(1770–1827)

Ludwig van Beethoven was born in Bonn, Germany. His father began teaching him to play the piano and violin when Beethoven was four years old. He later learned to play the harpsichord. Beethoven began losing his hearing early in his career. By the time he wrote "Missa Solemnis" and the "Ninth Symphony," he was totally deaf. Beethoven is considered one of the world's greatest composers, having written symphonies, string quartets, concertos, and an opera. Almost 200 years after his death, the music of Beethoven is still performed around the world.

I Love a Piano

Words and Music by IRVING BERLIN
Arranged by ROBERT W. SMITH

I love a pia - no, I love a pia - no, I love to hear some-bod - y play up-on a pia - no, a grand pi - an - o, it sim - ply car - ries me a - way. I know a fine way to treat a Stein - way. I love to run my fin - gers o'er the keys, the i - vo - ries. And with the ped - al I love to med-dle. Not on - ly mu - sic from Broad-

And with the ped - al I love to med-dle. Mu - sic,

The Versatile Piano

In the year 2000 the piano celebrated its 300 birthday. It was invented in Florence, Italy, in 170 by an Italian named Cristofori. Until then, tl harpsichord was the main keyboard instrument use, but it could produce only one dynamic lev While the harpsichord's strings were plucked, tl piano's strings were struck by a small hammer th allowed them to be played loudly or softly, depending on how tl performer pressed each key. The instrument was originally called pianoforte, meaning soft and loud, but was eventually shortened to pianc

Upon hearing of the piano, composers, such as Mozart and Beethoven, began writing music for it. Inventors added more and more notes to the keyboard to meet composers' requirements, until finally it was standardized to have 88 keys. Around the late 1700s a single-piece iron frame was incorporated into the design of the piano to allow it to be larger and create a sound that could carry throughout a large concert hall or above a symphony orchestra. This innovation allowed the piano to grow in popularity during the Romantic

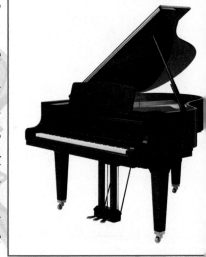

Era through the solo and concerto compositions of Chopin, Liszt, ar Brahms. The varied sound qualities capable of being made by the piar made it an important instrument for impressionist composers such Debussy and Ravel and for the modern compositional styles used Prokofiev and Gershwin.

By the late 1800s the piano was the instrument everyone wanted to have in their home. The piano roll was invented about this time. It was a device that could activate the piano keys automatically without having a person playing the instrument. This type of automated piano was called a player piano. As the piano grew in popularity, different and less formal styles of piano performance emerged. Scott Joplin helped make ragtime, an early form of jazz, a popular style of music in America around the early 1900s. The piano became an essential instrument for popular as well as concert music performance styles.

Innovations continued to be incorporated into keyboard instruments throughout the 1900s by, instead of making sounds acoustically, using electricity and, later, computer technology to generate piano-like sounds. By the 1980s digital technology had evolved so that keyboard instruments could create an amazing variety of sound qualities through a system called Music Instrument Digital Interface, or MIDI. By the 1990s computer technology was incorporated  into acoustic pianos. The Disklavier is an acoustic piano that is played by a computer. It is today's version of the old player piano.

The technological innovations of the last 300 years have helped make the piano the most versatile of music instruments. The piano has been a part of the development of every style of music performance since its invention, and it is played throughout the world. After reading about the development of the piano over time, what do you think the piano will be like in the future?

Square Piano by Francisco Florez

- **The keyboard of this piano contains three octaves. Do you think this is the same or different from today's pianos?**

- **Is this piano in a simple style or an ornamented style?**

- **How is this ornamentation similar to ornamentation in music?**

Harpsichord, London, 1743

- **How many keyboards are on this harpsichord?**

- **Do you suppose the notes on the higher keyboard sound the same as the notes on the lower keyboard? Why?**

- **How would you compare this harpsichord with the square piano on the left?**

Take Me Out to the Ball Game

Words by JACK NORWORTH
Music by ALBERT VON TILZER
Arranged by ROBERT W. SMITH

Take me out to the ball game.

Take me out with the crowd.

Buy me some pea - nuts and Crack - er Jack, I don't

care if we nev - er get back. Let me root, root, root for the

home team. If they don't win, it's a shame,____

____ for it's one, two, three strikes, you're

out at the old ball game.____

Pipe organ

The Organ

The organ in the church is called a pipe organ because it uses pipes of all sizes to create a variety of sounds. The pipe organ is sometimes called the "King of Instruments" because of the different kinds of sounds it can create. Church pipe organs have several hundred to more than a thousand pipes depending on the size of the church. Pipe organs have been played in churches for hundreds of years. Johann Sebastian Bach, who was born in 1685, played on a similar pipe organ in several churches in Germany where he lived.

The sound of the ballpark organ is made electronically. The organ was the first music instrument to become completely electronic in 1934. Electric circuits and amplifiers replaced the pipes. Because these electronic organs are so much smaller than pipe organs, they can be found in people's homes, churches, restaurants, ballparks, theaters, and small dance bands.

Musician plays large organ in Atlanta's Fox Theater

Ballpark

neighbor tone

A tone that travels a step above or below a tone before returning to the original tone

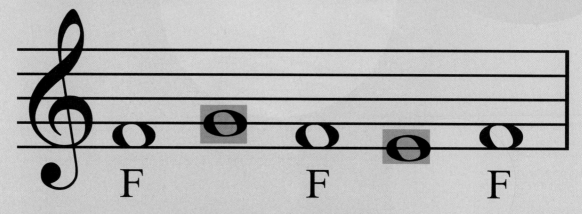

Find the **neighbor tone.**
What is its note name?

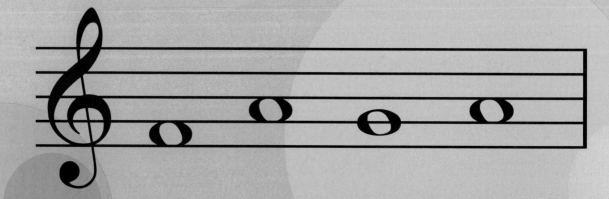

passing tone

A non-chord tone that travels in stepwise motion between two chord tones

F A C

Find the **passing tone.**
What is its note name?

root tone
The note on which the chord is built and named

seventh chord
A chord whose fourth tone (counting up from the root tone) is the seventh tone of the scale

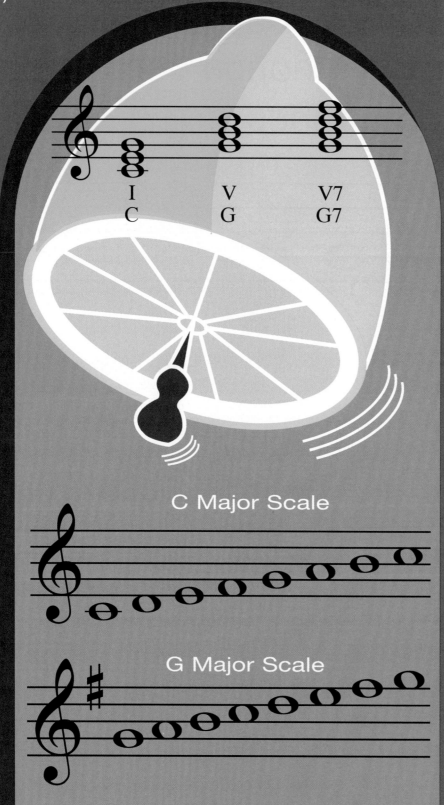

C Major Scale

G Major Scale

Play chords on highlighted sections.

Oranges and Lemons

TRADITIONAL ENGLISH SONG
Arranged by ARTIE ALMEIDA

baroque

A period of music between the years 1600 and 1750 characterized by the use of melodic ornamentation

classical

A period of music from about 1750 to 1825 characterized by concern for musical form, clarity, and balance

romantic

A period of music from the 1820's to the early 1900's characterized by dramatic contrasts and the expression of feeling

impressionist

A period of music from about 1890 to 1910 characterized by complex textures, unique harmonies, and the use of the whole-tone scale

modern

A period of twentieth-century music whose composers experimented with nontraditional harmonies, rhythms, and meters

1600
1650
1700
1750
1775
1800
1825
1850
1875
1900
1925
1950
1975
2000
presen

Johann Sebastian Bach 1685–1750

He wrote a large number of keyboard works and church music for various ensembles as well as a large amount of chamber music. His music is still very well known and often performed. He was the supreme master of counterpoint and every type of baroque music except opera.

Ludwig van Beethoven 1770–1827

His nine symphonies are orchestral masterpieces. He also wrote one opera, one mass, piano sonatas, and concerti and quite a number of chamber pieces for strings.

Johannes Brahms 1833–1897

A brilliant pianist in his youth, he composed mainly in classical forms, but he used many romantic harmonies. He wrote four symphonies, other orchestral pieces, instrumental chamber music, piano sonatas and other piano works, choral works, and numerous songs.

Claude Debussy 1862–1918

He developed an original writing style called impressionism and explored new possibilities for orchestral tone colors (sounds). Debussy wrote chamber, symphonic, and solo piano works and a famous music drama, *Pelleas et Melisande*.

Leonard Bernstein 1918–1990

In 1957, this American conductor and composer wrote a Broadway musical that was an updated version of *Romeo and Juliet*; it was called *West Side Story* and it blended classical and popular music. Bernstein was also the music director for the New York Philharmonic Orchestra for many years and a huge influence on classical music in the last half of the twentieth century.

J. S. Bach

Leonard Bernstein

Johannes Brahms

J. S. Bach

Bach was one of the most important composers in European history. He was a church musician all of his life, and people today still regularly sing and play his music in church. He did not play the piano until he was an old man, so most of his keyboard music was composed for the clavichord, a very popular keyboard instrument during the baroque era. In the baroque era lots of ornamentation was added to clothing and furniture. Baroque music was also very ornamented.

Johannes Brahms

Brahms is well known for his piano music, but he also composed beautiful symphonic and choral music. He composed during the romantic era. The romantic era was a time when people loved beautiful harmonies and melodies. They liked program music that told a story. Brahms' music is frequently performed today.

Leonard Bernstein

Bernstein was a famous twentieth-century composer who also wrote musical comedies. One of his most famous popular works is the musical *West Side Story*. He was also a recognized conductor. He conducted orchestras all over the world but is most closely associated with the New York Philharmonic Orchestra, one of the premier orchestras in the United States.

Rouen Cathedral at Sunset by Claude Monet

- **Does this painting look exactly like a cathedral?**

- **What makes *Rouen Cathedral at Sunset* look like an impressionist painting?**

- **What characteristics do this painting and impressonist music have in common?**

The Sunken Cathedral
by Claude Debussy

1. Look at the words and choose the ones that match what you are hearing.
2. When you finish listening, explain your choices to your classmates.
3. Which part of the music—beginning, middle, or end—matched each word?

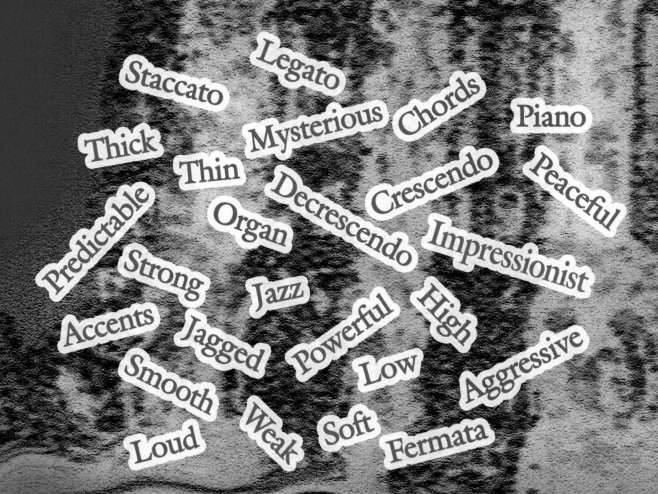

Legato
Staccato
Mysterious   Chords   Piano
Thick   Thin
Crescendo   Peaceful
Predictable   Decrescendo
Organ   Impressionist
Strong   Jazz
Accents   Powerful   High
Jagged
Smooth   Low   Aggressive
Loud   Weak   Soft   Fermata

diatonic scale

Seven tones in the order of the musical alphabet, starting on any tone, with the whole steps and half steps matching the pattern of the white keys on the piano

C D E F G A B C

whole-tone scale

A one-octave scale of six tones a whole step apart from each other

C D E F♯ G♯ A♯ C

Over the Rainbow

Music by HAROLD ARLEN
Lyric by E.Y. HARBURG
Arranged by MICHAEL STORY

146

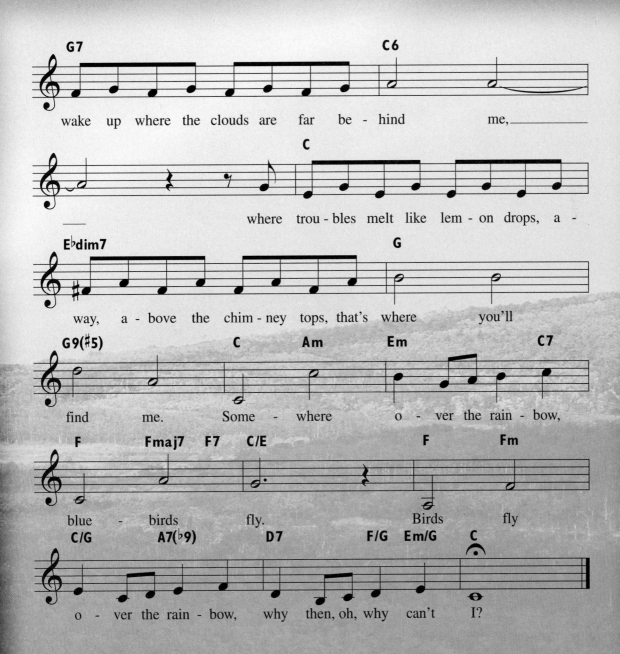

Harpsichord, 17th Century CE. French

Jaws by Gil Mayers

Two Girls at the Piano by Auguste Renoir

- **How are these three pieces of artwork the same?**

- **How are they different?**

- **Which artwork is impressionist?**

- **Which artwork is baroque?**

- **What era does *Jaws* represent?**

- **Match the musical arrangements of "Over the Rainbow" to the artwork of that era. In your journal, label the era for the art and music.**

- **Which artwork do you like best? Why?**

George Gershwin

George Gershwin's songs are some of the most lasting modern popular music written in the twentieth century. Gershwin died when he was very young. He is credited with being one of the first composers to merge jazz and classical music styles. One of his most famous works is the folk opera *Porgy and Bess*.

Tin Pan Alley

George Gershwin and Irving Berlin worked in an area of New York City called Tin Pan Alley. Since there was no air conditioning, the windows were all open, and people on the streets could hear the music of all the songwriters who worked in that part of the city. It was so noisy that some people said the music sounded as if someone were beating on a tin pan—thus the name Tin Pan Alley. Many songs by the composers of Tin Pan Alley are still popular today.

GERSHWIN® MEDLEY

(I Got Rhythm/Bidin' My Time/Strike Up the Band!)

Music and Lyrics by
GEORGE GERSHWIN and IRA GERSHWIN
Arranged by MICHAEL STORY

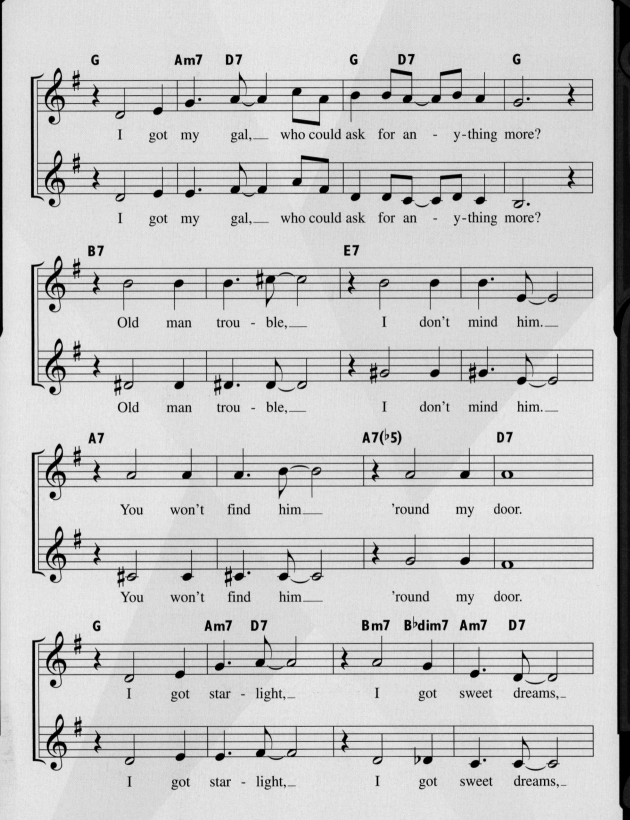

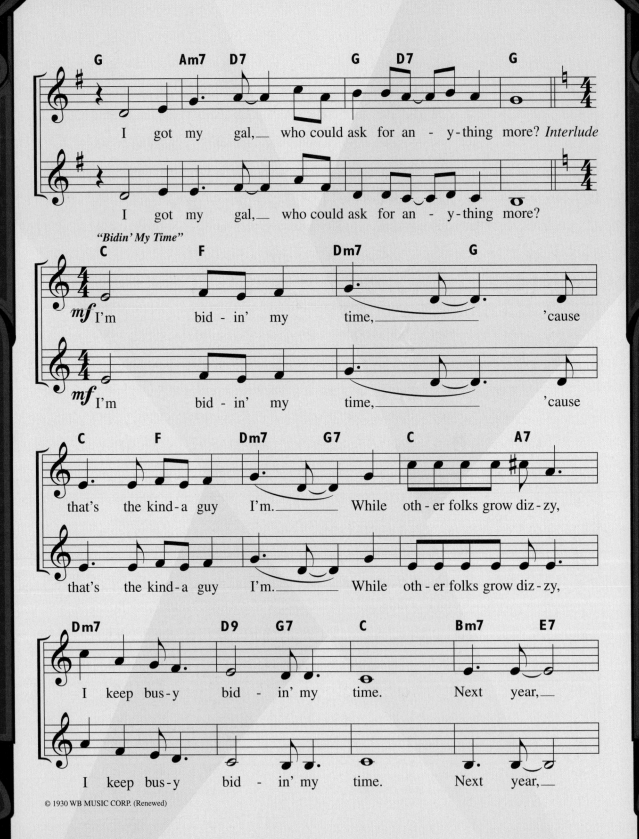

I got my gal,— who could ask for an-y-thing more? *Interlude*

I got my gal,— who could ask for an-y-thing more?

"Bidin' My Time"

mf I'm bid-in' my time,_____ 'cause

mf I'm bid-in' my time,_____ 'cause

that's the kind-a guy I'm._____ While oth-er folks grow diz-zy,

that's the kind-a guy I'm._____ While oth-er folks grow diz-zy,

I keep bus-y bid-in' my time. Next year,—

I keep bus-y bid-in' my time. Next year,—

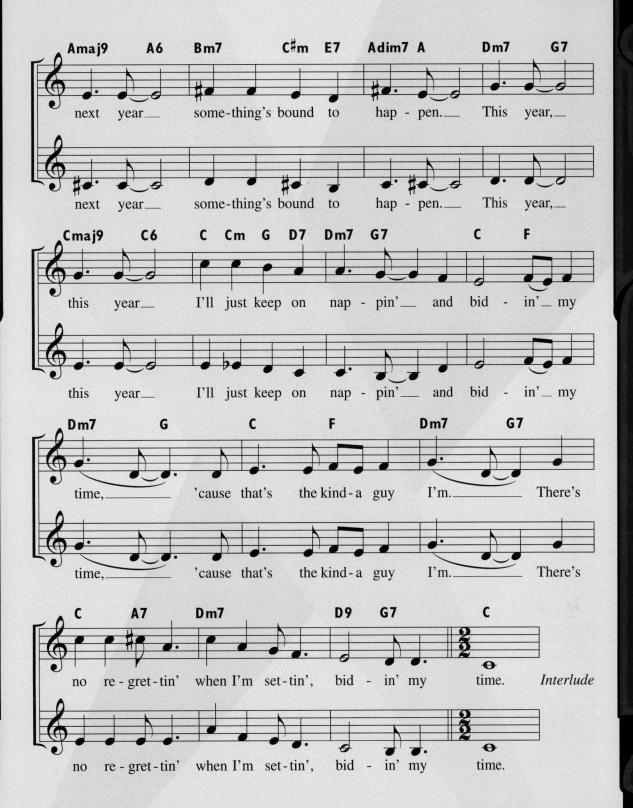

next year___ some-thing's bound to hap-pen.___ This year,___

next year___ some-thing's bound to hap-pen.___ This year,___

this year___ I'll just keep on nap-pin'___ and bid-in' my

this year___ I'll just keep on nap-pin'___ and bid-in' my

time,_____ 'cause that's the kind-a guy I'm.___ There's

time,_____ 'cause that's the kind-a guy I'm.___ There's

no re-gret-tin' when I'm set-tin', bid-in' my time. *Interlude*

no re-gret-tin' when I'm set-tin', bid-in' my time.

"Strike Up the Band!"

Let the drums roll out,_____ let the trum-pets call,_____

Shout!

f Boom boom boom! Ta - ta -

while the peo - ple shout,_____ "Strike up the

ra - ta - ta - ta - tat, Hoo - rah!

band!"_____ Hear the cym - bals ring,_____ call-ing

Tszing tszing tszing

one and all,_____ to the mar - tial swing,_____ strike up the

Ta - ta - ra - ta - ta - ta - tat, Yes, sir!

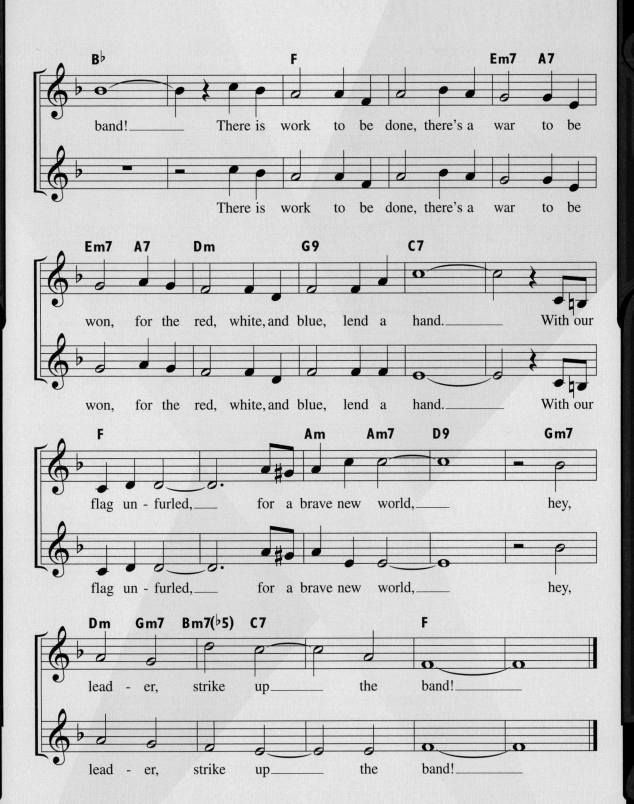

You've Got a Friend in Me

Words and Music by RANDY NEWMAN
Arranged by MICHAEL STORY

theme music

Music that is familiar because it is identified with a character, movie, TV show, radio program, or other production

Randy Newman

Randy Newman

(b. 1943)

Randy Newman was born in Los Angeles November 28, 1943. His uncles Alfred and Lionel were both noted film composers, and even his father, who was a doctor, wrote songs as a hobby. While studying music at UCLA, Randy became a professional songwriter and worked for a California publishing company.

His early influences were Bob Dylan, his visits to New Orleans, and traditional pop, gospel, and rhythm and blues. He also injects his sense of humor into his music.

Mr. Newman has written the musical scores for 17 movies, including *Monsters, Inc.*, *Toy Story* and *Toy Story 2*, *The Natural*, and *Seabiscuit*.

"You've Got a Friend in Me" was written for the movie *Toy Story*, and "If I Didn't Have You" from *Monsters, Inc.*, won him an Oscar in 2002 after 16 nominations.

Peter and the Wolf

Listen to the music and match the themes to the characters.

J. AQUINO   163

THEME MUSIC IN OUR LIVES

LOONEY TUNES, characters, names and all related indicia are trademarks of Warner Bros. © 2003.

Music Criteria

1. The music matches the chords of the accompaniment track.
2. The notation should be correct.
3. _____
4. _____

Your themes should fit the following guidelines:

- An eight-measure pattern that repeats except for the first and second endings.

- In the key of C major.

- Performed on mallet instruments and recorders and rhythm instruments that match the mood of your music.

- In 4/4 time.

- Use any rhythm patterns you think appropriately convey the mood of your story and that you can notate correctly.

- Match the **I, I, V7, I** chordal pattern.

Theme Music

The chord tones should be used on the first and third beats—the strong beats—of the measure. The passing and neighbor tones can be used on the second and fourth beats of the measure or on the second part of the first and third beats if you are using eighth or sixteenth notes.

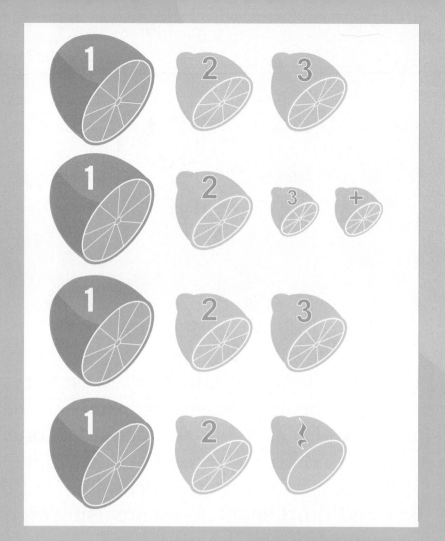

Oranges and Lemons

TRADITIONAL ENGLISH SONG
Arranged by ARTIE ALMEIDA

"Or - anges and lem - ons," say the bells of St.
"When will that be?"___ say the bells___ of
1   2   3   1   2   3 & 1   2   3

Clem - ents. "I owe you five far - things," say the
Step - ney. "I do not know,"___ says the
1   2   &   1   2   3   1   2   3 &

1 2
1 2 3
1 2 3 4 5
1 2 3 4 5

Careers in Music

Five Hat Forms by Kathi Packer

- **Do you think this is a serious or humorous painting?**

- **Is haberdasher a serious or humorous word? What is a haberdasher?**

- **How are the artwork *Five Hat Forms* and the composition "Take Five" similar?**

- **Are these hats grouped as 3 hats and 2 hats, or as 2 hats and 3 hats? Were the beats in "Take Five" grouped as 3 and 2, or as 2 and 3?**

Gospel singer performing at church

gospel music

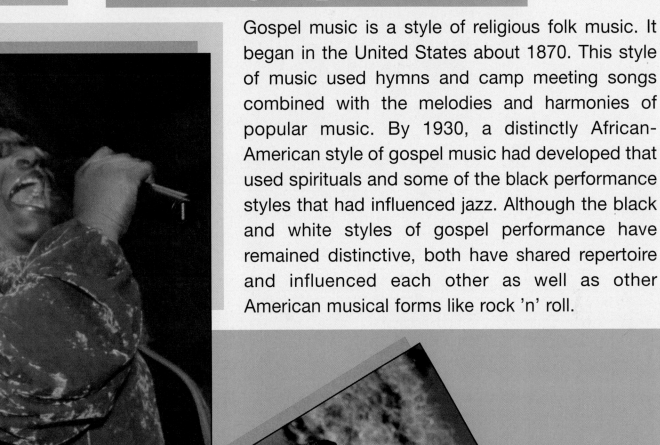

Gospel music is a style of religious folk music. It began in the United States about 1870. This style of music used hymns and camp meeting songs combined with the melodies and harmonies of popular music. By 1930, a distinctly African-American style of gospel music had developed that used spirituals and some of the black performance styles that had influenced jazz. Although the black and white styles of gospel performance have remained distinctive, both have shared repertoire and influenced each other as well as other American musical forms like rock 'n' roll.

Mahalia Jackson

Wade in the Water

TRADITIONAL GOSPEL SONG
Arranged by ROBERT W. SMITH

Gospel

Wade _____ in the wa - ter,

wade _____ in the wa - ter, chil - dren, wade _____ in the

wa - ter, God's gon - na trou - ble the

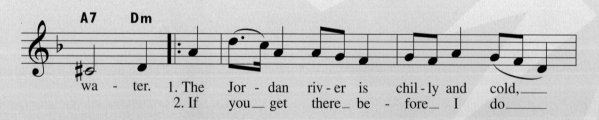

wa - ter. 1. The Jor - dan riv - er is chil - ly and cold, ____
2. If you get there be - fore ____ I do ____

God's gon-na trou-ble the wa - ter. It chills ____ my bod - y but
God's gon-na trou-ble the wa - ter. Tell all ____ my friends ____ I'm

Dave Brubeck

Dave Brubeck

(b. 1920)

Dave Brubeck was born in Concord, California. The Dave Brubeck Quartet began traveling in Brubeck's station wagon, with the string bass tied to the roof. A composer and pianist, he is a jazz legend. His West Coast cool jazz style characterized American jazz in the 1950s and 1960s. Brubeck has written two ballets, a musical, an oratorio, four cantatas, a mass, works for jazz combo and orchestra, and many solo piano pieces. Two of his well-known compositions are "Unsquare Dance," and "Blue Rondo à la Turk." "Take Five" was written by the quartet's saxophone player, Paul Desmond, but it is recognized as Dave Brubeck's theme song.

Rock 'n' Roll

Photo: Courtesy of STAR FILE INC.

Photo: Courtesy of HARRY GOODWIN/STAR FILE INC.

Bill Haley and the Comets

Elvis Presley

Booker T and the MGs

Rock 'n' roll is a style of American music that began in the mid-1950s. It is easy to dance to because it has a strong beat. This music is usually played by guitar, electric bass, piano, and drums. In 1955 the song "Rock Around the Clock" by Bill Haley and the Comets became a best-selling record, establishing rock 'n' roll as the most popular style of music in the United States. Other early rock 'n' roll stars were Jerry Lee Lewis, Chuck Berry, and Elvis Presley. Elvis was so popular that rock 'n' roll spread like wildfire around the world. Rock 'n' roll is still popular, although it has changed over the years and is included in the many different styles that make up today's popular music.

Photo: Courtesy of STAR FILE INC.

Photo: Courtesy of STAR FILE INC.

Fats Domino

Little Richard

Rock 'n' Stroll

By TIMOTHY S. BROPHY

Elvis Presley

Elvis Presley

(1935–1977)

Elvis Aaron Presley was born in Mississippi and moved to Memphis, Tennessee, in 1948. He began his career by singing hymns and gospel tunes with his parents at concerts and state fairs. His parents bought him his first guitar when he was 11 years old. He became known as the King of Rock and Roll with songs such as "Jailhouse Rock," "Hound Dog," "Blue Suede Shoes," "All Shook Up," and many more. After his death, Elvis's home in Memphis, called Graceland, became a shrine to his memory.

Recorder Review

Can you remember the fingerings for these notes?

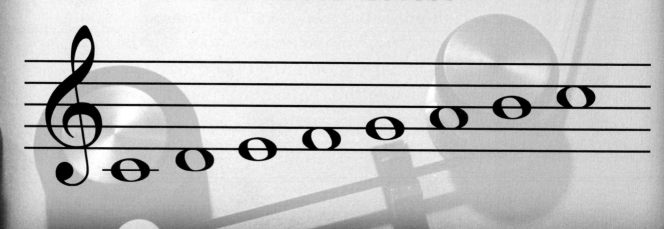

FWD   STOP   PLAY   RECORD

LO   MED   HI   ← MVC →

Review these fingerings:

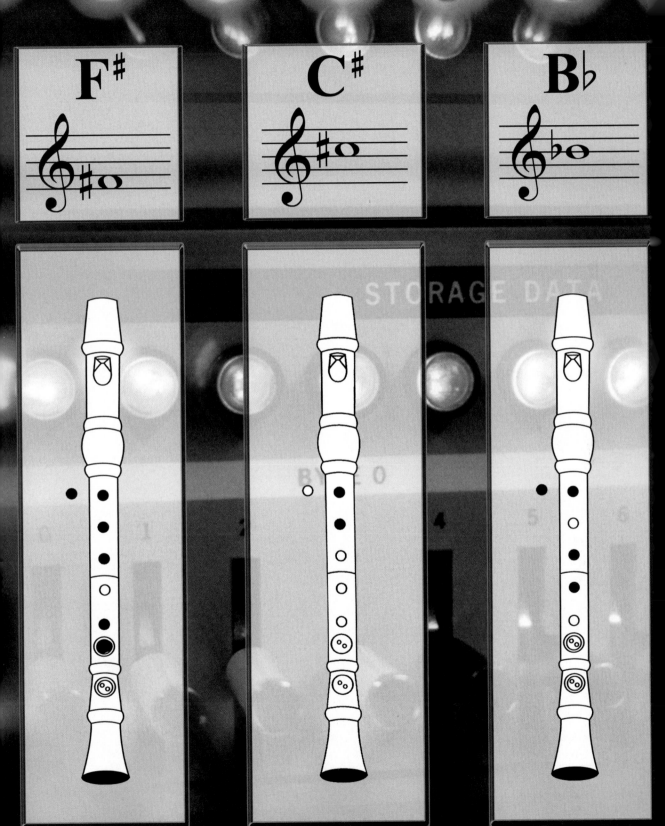

beach music

An American musical style of the
1960s that started on the beaches of
North and South Carolina

194

Wiped-Out Recorders

Play along with "Wipe Out"!

Words and Music by The Surfaris
Arranged by MICHAEL STORY

MOTOWN

The Supremes

Stevie Wonder

The Four Tops

Diana Ross with Berry Gordy

196

MOTOWN RECORDS

was a small company that became a big force in the music industry. Motown was started by Berry Gordy, Jr., who was born in Detroit, Michigan in 1929. After serving in the army, Gordy began writing and producing songs. Over the years, he produced many groups and artists that became famous. Listed below are some of these stars and a few of their hit songs that you might know:

Marvin Gaye: "I Heard It Through the Grapevine"
Jackson 5: "ABC" and "I'll Be There"
Martha and the Vandellas: "Heat Wave"
The Miracles: "Shop Around," featuring Smokey Robinson
The Supremes (with Diana Ross): "Baby Love" and "Stop! In the Name of Love"
Stevie Wonder: "My Cherie Amour" and "I Just Called to Say I Love You"
The Temptations: "My Girl"

198

Bob Dylan

(b. 1941)

Bob Dylan was born Robert Allen Zimmerman, grew up in Minnesota, and lives in New York. He is a singer and songwriter who mixes folk, country, blues, and rock styles. His music was very influential during the youth movement of the 1960s. Some of his most well-known songs include "The Times They Are A-Changin'," "Like a Rolling Stone," and "All Along the Watchtower." He also wrote and performed "Knocking on Heaven's Door," which became a number-one hit in 1973. The film *Don't Look Back* is a documentary of his 1965 rock tour.

Blowin' in the Wind

Words and Music by BOB DYLAN
Arranged by MICHAEL STORY

Recorder descant

mf

Vocal

mf How man-y roads must a man walk_ down be-

fore you call him a man? Yes 'n'

how man-y seas must a white dove_ sail be-

fore she sleeps in the sand? Yes 'n'

how man - y times must the can - non - balls___ fly be -

fore they're for - ev - er___ banned? The

fa   fa   mi   re   re   mi   mi   mi   re   do   do

an - swer, my friend, is blow-in' in the wind, the

fa   fa   mi   re   re   do   ti₁   do

an - swer is blow-in' in the wind.

descant
A part often sung or played
above the melody

Art Garfunkel and Paul Simon

Simon and Garfunkel

Simon and Garfunkel began performing together (as Tom and Jerry) when they were 13. In 1957, at 16 years old they had their first hit record, "Hey, Schoolgirl." Their two-part vocal harmony was modeled after their biggest early influence, the Everly Brothers. As Simon and Garfunkel, they were one of the most successful musical acts of the 1960s. Their songs "The Sound of Silence," "Mrs. Robinson," "Bridge Over Troubled Water," and "Scarborough Fair" were huge hits and have become symbolic of the music and culture of that era. Simon and Garfunkel's reunion concert in 1981 in Central Park (NY) drew more than half a million fans.

Paul Simon

(b. 1941)

Paul Frederic Simon was born in Newark, New Jersey, but his family moved to Forest Hills, New York, soon after he was born. Paul majored in music at New York University and English at Queens College. For three decades, since the break-up of Simon and Garfunkel, Paul has gone on to record and produce some of the most successful albums in popular music history, including *Still Crazy After All These Years, One Trick Pony, Graceland, Rhythm of the Saints,* and *You're the One.* In 2003, Paul was nominated for an Academy Award® for his song "Father and Daughter" from *The Wild Thornberrys Movie.*

Arthur Garfunkel

(b. 1941)

Arthur (Art) Ira Garfunkel was born in Forest Hills, New York. He studied mathematics at New York University and architecture at Columbia University. Since the break-up of Simon and Garfunkel, Art has been an actor, an author, and a producer. He has had several hit songs, including "I Only Have Eyes for You," "(What a) Wonderful World," and "Since I Don't Have You."

Martin Luther King Speaking at Selma Rally

- Protest marches and rallies are peaceful ways to fight injustice and are demonstrations of expressions and emotions.

- This is a photo of a civil rights rally.

- Who is the man on the right side of the photo?

We Shall Overcome

TRADITIONAL SPIRITUAL
Arranged by MICHAEL STORY

We shall o-ver-come, _____ we shall o-ver- come, _____ we shall o-ver-come some - day. _____ Oh, _____ deep in my heart I do be-lieve that we shall o-ver-come some - day. We shall live in peace, _____ we shall live in

"I Have a Dream!"

Stevie Wonder

Stevie Wonder

(b. 1950)

Stevie Wonder was born in Saginaw, Michigan, as Steveland Judkins. Although he was born blind, Wonder began to learn to play the piano when he was seven. By the age of nine, he could play the drums and harmonica. Wonder began recording when he was only 11 years old and quickly became one of Motown's finest artists. Some of his songs are "I Just Called to Say I Love You," "For Once in My Life," and "My Cherie Amour." Stevie Wonder was inducted into the Rock and Roll Hall of Fame in 1989.

FOR OR AGAINST

The late 1960s was a period of unrest marked by protests **against** the Vietnam War and movements **for** peace and love. Music became a powerful tool for expressing these messages. Songs such as "San Francisco" and "Woodstock" became anthems for the peace-and-love movement, while "Ohio" and "Fortunate Son" expressed the anger and frustration of the anti-war movement against the Vietnam War.

FOR

"San Francisco" by John Phillips

If you're going to San Francisco
Be sure to wear some flowers in
* your hair.*
If you're going to San Francisco,
You're going to meet some gentle
* people there.*

SAN FRANCISCO
© 1967, 1970 Universal-MCA Music Publishing

AGAINST

"Ohio" by Neil Young

Tin soldiers and Nixon coming,
We're finally on our own.
This summer I hear the drumming,
Four dead in Ohio.

OHIO
© 1970 Broken Arrow Music Corporation

A Sunday on La Grande Jatte—1884 by Georges Seurat

- **What is the setting of this painting?**

- **What different things do you see?**

- **Is it a bright sunny day or a rainy day?**

- **How do you know?**

- **What is the style of this painting?**

Park Near Lucerne (1938) by Paul Klee

Do you see the park in this artwork?

How is this park similar to the one on page 214?

How is it different?

Do you think the dates of these works of art affect their style? How?

Which of the two do you like best? Why?

James Taylor

James Taylor

(b. 1948)

James Taylor's family traces its history back through several generations of a New England seafaring family. His father, a former seaman himself, was dean of the University of North Carolina Medical School. Taylor's mother was a classically trained singer, and his siblings—Alex, Livingston, and Kate—were all successful musicians in their own right. James was part of the folk revolution of the 1960s and 1970s, and his gentle fusion of folk and rock, with a touch of gospel and soul, set the standard for generations of singer-songwriters, including modern artists such as Jewel, John Mayer, and Norah Jones. His songs have been re-recorded by many artists. Even Pat Metheny, the groundbreaking modern jazz guitarist, paid tribute to Taylor with his song "James" from his album *Offramp*. James Taylor's first recording was released in 1970 and contained songs that are still popular, such as "Sweet Baby James," "Country Road," and "Fire and Rain." In 2000, James Taylor was inducted into both the Rock and Roll Hall of Fame and the Songwriters Hall of Fame.

You've Got a Friend

Words and Music by CAROLE KING
Arranged by MICHAEL STORY

ritardando
(rit., ritard.)
To gradually slow down the tempo

Wade in the Water

TRADITIONAL GOSPEL SONG
Arranged by ROBERT W. SMITH

Gospel

Wade in the wa - ter,

wade in the wa - ter, chil - dren, wade in the

wa - ter, God's gon - na trou - ble the

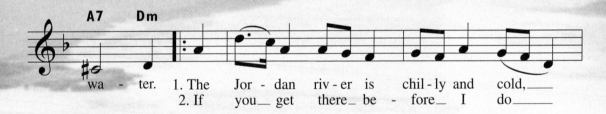

wa - ter. 1. The Jor - dan riv - er is chil - ly and cold,
2. If you get there be - fore I do

God's gon-na trou-ble the wa - ter. It chills my bod - y but
God's gon-na trou-ble the wa - ter. Tell all my friends I'm

Take 6

Take 6

Take 6 is an all male a cappella singing group that performs gospel music. The group was started by Claude McKnight as the Gentlemen's Estate Quartet in 1980 at Oakwood College in Huntsville, Alabama. The other members of Take 6 are Alvin Chea, Cedric Carl Dent, Joey Kibble, Mark Winston Kibble, and David Thomas. Alvin and David live in the Los Angeles area. The others live in Nashville.

acoustic

Musical instruments not requiring external electrical power to make sound

electronic

Musical instruments requiring external electrical power to make sound

Acoustic to Electronic

Acoustic is a word that comes from Greek, meaning "to hear." Acoustics is a way of making sounds that are not changed electrically. The use of acoustic instruments was popular before the birth of electronic instruments.

Electronic instruments have been around a long time. Electronic music is used in rock 'n' roll, rhythm and blues, pop, and blues. Even classical performers began using electronics. It got little attention, however, until Wendy Carlos did a recording in 1968 called *Switched-On Bach.* The Bach pieces on this recording were performed on a synthesizer that made sounds from a computerized electronic keyboard.

The many ways that technology could be used to make and combine previously unheard sounds was fascinating. In the 1970s, more performances included electronic music. A lot of the music written for dancing was electronic. Electronic keyboards were much more portable than pianos and never needed tuning. They became the keyboard of choice for many groups.

Stayin' Alive

We Are the World

Words and Music by
MICHAEL JACKSON
and LIONEL RITCHIE
Arranged by ROBERT W. SMITH

Refrain

We are the world,__ we are the chil - dren, we are the ones__ to make a bright - er day, so let's__ start giv - ing. There's a choice we're mak - ing,__ we're sav - ing our__ own lives,__ it's true,__ we make a bet - ter day,__ just you__ and me.

Quincy Jones

Quincy Jones

(b. 1933)

Quincy Jones was born March 14, 1933, in Chicago and brought up in Seattle. He is a successful composer, record producer, artist, film producer, arranger, conductor, instrumentalist, TV producer, and record company executive.

He has blended pop, soul, hip-hop, jazz, classical, African, and Brazilian music in every medium, including records, live performance, movie, and television.

While in junior high school, Quincy began studying trumpet and sang in a gospel quartet. His musical studies continued at Berklee College of Music in Boston. In 1957, he decided to continue his musical education by studying with Nadia Boulanger, who tutored composers such as Leonard Bernstein and Aaron Copland.

Quincy has received numerous awards and honors. In fact, he is the all-time most nominated Grammy artist, with a total of 79 Grammy nominations.

His theme from the hit TV series "Ironside" was the first synthesizer-based pop theme song. He was the producer and conductor of the historic "We Are the World" recording (the best-selling single of all time) and Michael Jackson's solo albums *Off the Wall, Bad,* and *Thriller* (the best-selling album of all time). Quincy Jones Entertainment (QJE) produced NBC Television's "Fresh Prince of Bel Air," UPN's "In the House," and Fox Television's "Mad TV."

Reflecting on the changes in pop music over the years, Quincy says, "If there are any common denominators, they are spirit and musicality. I go for the music that gives me goose bumps, music that touches my heart and my soul."

We Are the World

MICHAEL JACKSON
and LIONEL RITCHIE
Arranged by ROBERT W. SMITH

Verse 1

all a part__ of_____ God's great big fam - i - ly__ and the

Refrain

truth, you know, love is all we need.__ We are the world,_

we are the chil - dren, we are the ones_

__ to make a bright-er day,_ so let's_ start giv - ing. There's a

choice we're mak - ing,___ we're sav - ing our__ own lives,_ it's true,_

__ we make a bet - ter day,_ just you__ and me.__

Carlos Santana

Impact
of Culture
on Music

Angélique Kidjo

Bob Marley

Much of the music written and performed today is influenced by cultures around the world. The musicians combine current trends with the styles, rhythms, and languages of their own cultures.

As the popularity of their music grows, so does the impact of these musicians' cultures. What cultures have influenced the music of these artists?

Celine Dion

Ricky Martin

George Benson

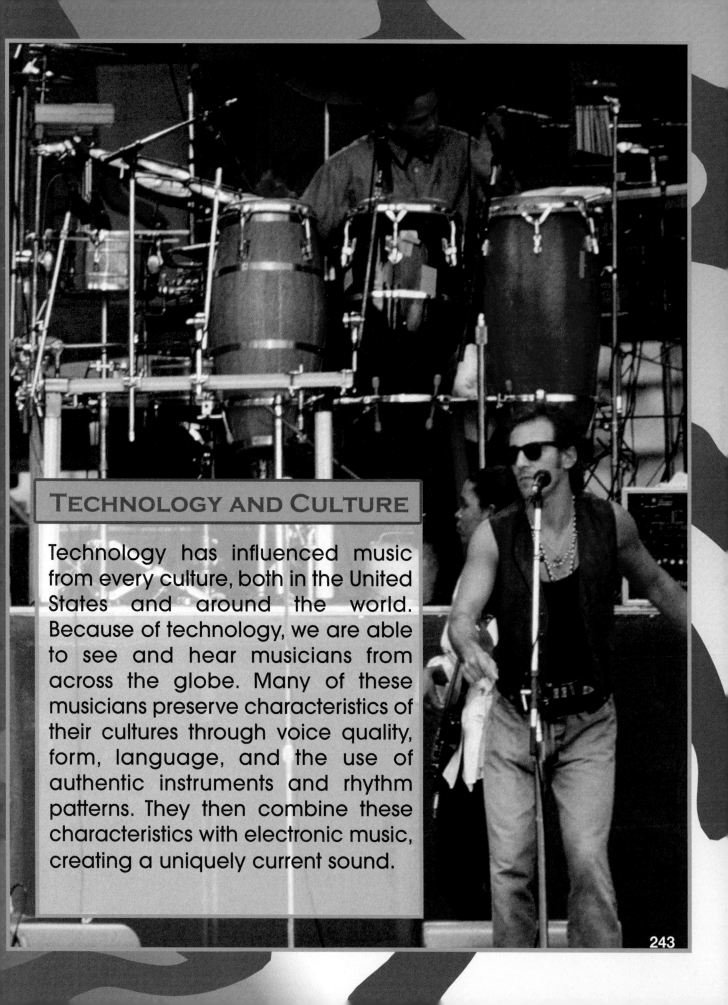

TECHNOLOGY AND CULTURE

Technology has influenced music from every culture, both in the United States and around the world. Because of technology, we are able to see and hear musicians from across the globe. Many of these musicians preserve characteristics of their cultures through voice quality, form, language, and the use of authentic instruments and rhythm patterns. They then combine these characteristics with electronic music, creating a uniquely current sound.

Children of the World...

Words and Music by
BRANDON BARNES
and ROBERT W. SMITH

Verse

Gently

Can you hear it in our hearts? A sin-gle

rhy-thm set a-part, beat-ing pure and in-no-cent e-ven

through the dark. Red and yel-low, black and white, all the same

in our eyes. If we come to-geth-er, we can

Refrain

bright-en this world. We can sing with one voice to-geth-

-er if we make a choice. We can dream, if you lis-ten, you can hear

_____ us._____ We're the chil - dren of___ the world.___

Verse

E - ven though___ we ap - pear small,_____ in our hearts___

___ we're stand - ing tall.___ And we know____ we're the fu - ture___ of to-

mor - row.___ E - ven we___ see___ the need___ for peace,_

___ for u - ni - ty,___ and if___ we come_ to - geth - er,___ we can

Refrain

bright-en this world.____ We can sing____ with one voice_ to - geth-

- er if___ we make_ a choice.__ We can dream,____ we can fly____ on the wings_

___ of im - ag - i - na - tion.___ We can sing____ with one voice to - geth-

- er if___ we make___ a choice. We can dream,___ if you lis - ten,___ you can hear___

___ us.___ We're the chil - dren of___ the world,

...of the world! We can sing___

___ with one voice___ to-geth - er if___ we make___ a choice. We can dream,___

___ we can fly_____ on the wings___ of im-ag - i - na - tion.___

We are___ the chil - dren,___ chil - dren of___ the world.

We are___ the chil - dren,___ chil-dren of___ the world.

We are___ the chil - dren,___ chil - dren of the world!_____

Lift Every Voice and Sing

By JAMES WELDON JOHNSON
and J. ROSAMOND JOHNSON
Arranged by ROBERT W. SMITH

Lift ev-'ry voice and sing,
till earth and heav - en ring,
ring with the har - mo - nies of
lib - er - ty. Let our re - joic -
ing rise high as the lis -
t'ning_____ skies, let it re - sound
loud as the roll - ing sea._____

Sing a song full of the faith that the dark past has taught us. Sing a song full of the hope that the pres-ent has brought_____ us. Fac-ing the ris - ing sun of our new day be - gun, let us march on till vic-to- ry_____ is won._____

Can you name th

se instruments?

Show What

minor scale

whole-tone scale

melodic rhythm

"Wade in the Water"

bass

whole step

syncopa

major scale

"Take 5"

mezzo forte (mf)

"Blowin' in the Wind"

diatonic scale

interval

eighth

rest

octave

sixteenth

largo

steady beat

quarter

YOU KNOW

"Blue Suede Shoes"

crescendo

mezzo piano (mp)

half step

decrescendo

pianissimo (pp)

accompaniment

piano (p)

forte (f)

keyboard

"The Star Spangled Banner"

woodwind

electronic

alto

brass

song lyrics

percussion

mood

tenor

soprano

Recorder Review

Can you remember the fingerings for these notes?

Part 1

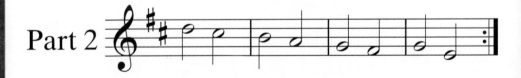
Part 2

Part 3

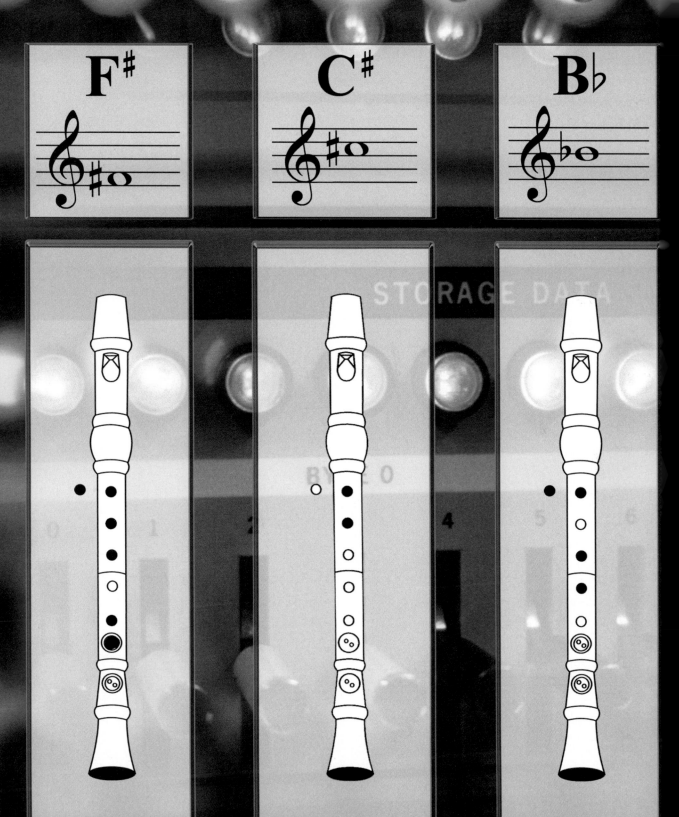

The Star Spangled Banner

The Star Spangled Banner

Words by FRANCIS SCOTT KEY
Arranged by ROBERT W. SMITH

gal - lant - ly stream - ing? And the rock - et's red

glare, the bombs burst - ing in air, gave

proof through the night that our flag was still

there. Oh say! Does that__ star span - gled

ban - ner__ yet__ wave,__ o'er the land__ of the

free and the home of the brave?

There are many composers
of music history. These are

Rom

ca. 182

Richard
Wagner

Franz Lisz

Frederic
Chopin

Johanne
Brahm

Classical
ca. 1750–1825

Ludwig van
Beethoven

Wolfgang Amadeus Mozart

Franz Josef Haydn

Baroque
ca. 1600–1750

George Frideric Handel

Johann Sebastian Bach

Antonio Vivaldi

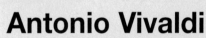
ca. is short for *circa*, meaning "around, about, or approximately."

who wrote in each period

only a few.

antic

-1910

Impressionist

ca. 1890–1910

Maurice Ravel

Claude Debussy

Modern

ca. 1890–

Leonard Bernstein

John Williams

George Gershwin

Igor Stravinsky

Charles Ives

259

Show What You Know

BAROQUE   Classical   Ro

antic   *Impressionist*   **Modern**

261

Blue Man Group

263

264

265

Glossary

a cappella	Singing without instrumental accompaniment
AB form	A musical form consisting of two different sections
ABA form	A musical form in which the first section (A) is repeated after the second section (B)
accelerando	Getting faster
accidental	A sharp, flat, or natural symbol before a note that is not found in the key signature (page 8)
accompaniment	A supporting part for singers or instrumentalists; a part that supports the melody or main part (page 130)
acoustic	Any musical instrument not requiring external electrical power to make sound (page 227)
African-American spiritual	A style of song developed by African-American slaves, usually religious, with elements of African rhythms and biblical texts
arco	To play a string instrument with a bow rather than by plucking
arpeggio	The notes of a chord sounded one after the other, from low to high or high to low (page 44)
audience	A group of people who listen to or watch a live performance
audience etiquette	The rules for proper behavior during a live performance
ballad	A song that tells a story
band	An instrumental ensemble, usually made up of wind and percussion instruments and no string instruments
barbershop	An American style of a cappella singing in close harmony
barbershop quartet	A group of four persons who sing music in barbershop style
baroque	A period of music from 1600 to 1750 characterized by the use of melodic ornamentation and forward motion over a consistent, unchanging pulse; the main composers include Bach, Handel, and Vivaldi. (page 138)
beach music	A 1960s original musical style of American rhythm & blues and rock 'n' roll that originated on the beaches of the Carolinas (page 194)
big band	A jazz ensemble (jazz band) that traditionally includes five saxes, four trumpets, four trombones, and a rhythm section of piano, bass, drums, and sometimes guitar.
bluegrass	A style of music that originated in the southern United States that contains rapid tempos, jazz-like improvisation, and emphasis on stringed instruments such as the banjo, guitar, mandolin, and fiddle
blues	A style of music that grew out of southern American songs, using only three chords, and "mi" and "ti" are usually flatted
body percussion	Sounds that are produced by actions such as clapping, snapping, and stomping
bossa nova	A Brazilian musical style developed in the late '50s from the samba rhythm mixed with elements of the cool jazz style. The term bossa nova comes from the Portuguese language and means "new style."
Broadway	An area in New York City where there are many theatres that present plays and musicals (see *musical*); this word is also used to describe the musical style of the songs in the musicals presented in the theatres in this area
call-and-response	A performance style or musical form in which a leader's solo (the call) is followed by an answer phrase performed by a group (the response)
canon	A musical form in which the same music is performed by two or more persons beginning at different times so they overlap (page 118)
cantata	A story, usually sacred, set to music and sung by a choir and soloists and accompanied by an orchestra
chant	A text recited in rhythm
chord	Three or more notes sounded at the same time (page 44)

chorus/choir	A group of singers
classical	A period of music from about 1750 to 1825 characterized by clarity and balance; simple, unornamented melodies; and straightforward, conventional harmonies and form; the main composers include Haydn and Mozart (page 138)
composed song	Music written by one or more persons
composer	A person who writes music
conductor	A person who directs a group of musicians
countermelody	A second melody that is performed along with the main melody (page 66)
descant	A part often played or sung above the melody (page 203)
diatonic scale	Seven tones in the order of the musical alphabet, starting on any tone, with the whole steps and half steps matching the pattern of white keys on the piano; can be major or minor (page 145)
diction	Pronouncing words correctly and clearly when speaking or singing
Dixieland	A style of instrumental jazz that was born in New Orleans around 1900
downbeat	The first beat of a measure, often stressed
downward	Melodic direction toward lower sounding pitches
dress rehearsal	The final rehearsal before performing for an audience (page 73)
duet	A performance by two people, with or without accompaniment (page 52)
duple meter	Meter based on macrobeats that travel in groups of two
dynamics	One of the ways of making music expressive, these are the levels of loud and soft in a musical work
echo	The exact imitation of a given phrase, sound, or pattern
electronic	Any musical instrument requiring external electrical power to make sound (page 227)
ensemble	A group of musicians performing together
expressive	A way of performing music that shows mood or feeling
fast	Quick
fifth	The interval of five scale tones, counting the first and the last tones (page 116)
first ending	The first alternate ending to a repeated section (page 108)
folk song	A song passed down from generation to generation that most people learn by hearing others sing it
form	The way a musical composition is organized
fourth	The interval of four scale tones, counting the first and the last tones (page 116)
free canon	A musical form in which different versions of the same music are performed by two or more persons beginning at different times so they overlap (page 118)
gospel	A style of religious folk music (page 177)
half step	The smallest interval between two tones; the interval from any tone to the closest tone above or below it (page 27)
harmony	Two or more musical tones sounding at the same time (page 116)
high	A sound that is in the upper range or register of an instrument or voice
impressionism	A style of music from about 1890 to about 1910 characterized by the use of complex textures, unique harmonies, and the whole tone scale to create a special mood and setting; the main composers include Debussy and Ravel (page 139)
improvise (improvisation)	To create and perform music, speech, or movement on the spot (page 15)
interlude	In some musical forms, music that connects the larger sections
interval	The distance between two pitches (page 27)
introduction	A section of music at the beginning of a composition that sets the mood, style, and tempo of the music that follows (page 45)
jazz	A style of music originating in the twentieth century in New Orleans that combined elements of European, American, and African music. It is an improvisational, expressive style of music characterized by syncopated rhythms and blue notes.
key signature	The group of sharps or flats placed to the right of the clef on a musical staff to identify the key
leading tone	The tone that leads upward to the home tone, often the solfège note "ti"

ledger line	A short horizontal line added to the top or the bottom of a staff for notes too high or too low to be shown on the five-line staff; extends the lines and spaces (page 59)
legato	To perform notes in a smooth, connected manner (page 47)
long tone	A tone that is not short and that sounds a for a long time
loud	Not quiet
low	A sound that is in the bottom range or register of an instrument or voice
lullaby	Quiet music that is usually used to rock a baby to sleep
lyrics	The words of a song (page 24)
macrobeat	The steady beat or heartbeat of the music; the basic beat in a rhythm pattern
major scale	A diatonic scale with half steps between the third and fourth and the seventh and eighth tones (page 27)
mallet	A special stick with a round ball on one end used to play a percussion instrument
march	Music with a strong steady beat for moving
mariachi	A traditional style of music in Mexico, consisting of strings (guitars and violins), trumpets, and singers
measure	In musical notation, a group of beats separated by bar lines
melodic direction	The upward, downward, or repeated movement of tones in melodies
melodic rhythm	The pattern of sounds and silences in a melody; in songs, this is often the same as the rhythm of the words
melody	A series of pitches that creates the tune of a piece of music
meter	The repeated pattern of beats in a musical work
microbeat	The even division of the macrobeat
minor scale	A diatonic scale with half steps between the second and third and the fifth and sixth tones (page 48)
modern	A period of music history beginning in the early 1900s characterized by melodic and harmonic experimentation; major composers include Stravinsky and Bernstein (page 139)
mood	The way a composer, artist, or writer wants you to feel when you hear their music, see their art, or read their book, story, or poem
music criteria	Standards by which music and performance are evaluated (page 73)
musical	A play that includes popular songs and dance to help tell the story
neighbor tone	In melodies, a tone that travels a step above or below a tone before returning to the original tone (page 134)
notation	The written notes and symbols used to represent music on paper (page 13)
octave	An interval that spans the distance from one tone to the tone eight notes above or below it with the same name
opera	A drama set to music, usually sung throughout, featuring a combination of music, drama, scenery, and costumes
orchestra	A large group of musicians playing string, brass, woodwind, and percussion instruments
ornamentation	A note or group of notes that embellish or decorate the melody (page 119)
ostinato	A short musical pattern (melody or rhythm) that is repeated throughout all or part of a musical work (page 98)
passing tone	In melodies or chord sequences, a non-chord tone that travels in stepwise motion between two chord tones (page 135)
patriotic music	Music that helps us express our love for our country
pattern	A series of pitches, sounds, silences, or musical forms that repeat
pentatonic	Any five-tone scale ("do," "re," "mi," "sol," and "la") or music that is based on that five-tone scale
percussionist	One who plays percussion instruments (page 63)

personal repertoire	The collection of songs and musical works that a person can identify and perform (page 25)
phrase	A musical thought or idea
piano	A keyboard instrument that sounds when the keys are struck by the fingers, which causes a hammer to strike a string that is tuned to a specific pitch
pitch	A specific musical tone
pitched	A category of musical instruments that are able to produce specific musical tones or can be used to play melodies (page 34)
pizzicato	To play a string instrument by plucking the string rather than using the bow
polyrhythm	Two or more rhythms performed at the same time (page 98)
refrain	In a song, a section of music, sung or played, that is repeated between verses
relative minor	The scale that begins on the sixth tone or "la" of the major scale with the same key signature (page 48)
repeated pattern	A pattern that occurs several times
repeated tone	Tones that are the same and occur more than once
resonate	To sound through vibration
rest	A symbol that indicates a silent unit of time
rhythm	The pattern of sounds and silences in music (the duration or length of time notes are sounded)
rhythm of the words	The pattern of sounds and silences in the words to a song or poem; in songs, this is often the same as the melodic rhythm
ritardando	To gradually slow down the tempo, abbreviated as *ritard.* or *rit.* (page 221)
rock 'n' roll	An American musical style originating in the 1950s characterized by driving rhythms and performed by one or more vocalists and a band including drum set, guitar, piano, and bass
romantic	A period of music from approximately the 1820s through the early 1900s characterized by dramatic dynamic and rhythmic contrasts and complex harmonic structure to tell a musical story or convey an emotion; the main composers include Chopin, Brahms, and Wagner (page 138)
rondo	A musical form in which the first section is repeated several times with a different section in between, such as ABACA and ABACADA
root tone	The note upon which a chord is built and named (page 136)
samba	A popular Brazilian dance rhythm usually felt in two and heavily syncopated
scale	A series of tones (moving upward or downward) that presents the pitches of a key, beginning and ending on the home tone of that key.
score	The written form of a musical composition (page 42)
second ending	The second alternate ending to a repeated section (page 108)
setting	The time (when), place (where), and action (who or what) in which music, art, or a story occurs or develops
seventh chord	A chord whose fourth tone is the interval of a seventh above the root tone, or the seventh tone of the scale (page 136)
short tone	A tone that is not long and sounds only a brief time
skip	The distance from one tone to a tone that is more than a step away from it (up or down)
singing voice	The voice we use to share melodies and songs
slow	Not quick; unhurried
soft	Quiet
solfège	Syllable names ("do," "re," "mi,"" fa," "sol," "la," "ti") for tones of a scale
solo	A performance by one person, with or without accompaniment (page 52)
sound source	The instrument or device making a sound; the origin of sound
speaking voice	The voice we use to say words and make other sounds that are not melodies or songs

steady beat	The even pulse of music; the heartbeat or macrobeat of music
step	The distance from one tone to the tone next to it (up or down)
style	The special way something is done, created, or performed
syncopa	A vocalization for a syncopated rhythm pattern
syncopation	Placing an accent on a normally weak or unaccented part of a beat
tempo	The speed of the beat
texture	The musical quality that is created by layering different voices, instruments, melodies, and harmonies
theme and variations	A musical form in which a melody (the theme) is presented and then varied musically for the remainder of the work
theme music	Music that is familiar because it is identified with a character, movie, TV show, radio program, or other production
tone	The sound of a specific musical pitch
tone color	The sound that is special or unique to a voice or an instrument
transpose	To write or perform music in a key other than the original or given key (page 66)
triple meter	Meter based on macrobeats that travel in groups of three
tutti	All perform; everyone performs together
unpitched	A category of musical instruments (mostly percussion) that are unable to produce a specific tone and cannot play a melody (page 34)
upbeat	The last beat of a measure, leading to the downbeat
upward	Melodic direction toward higher sounding pitches
verse	In a song, the sections of music with the same melody but different words each time and usually separated by a refrain
whole step	A musical interval equal to two half steps (page 27)
whole-tone scale	A series of six tones, each a whole step apart (page 145)
zydeco	A style of music originating with the Louisiana Cajun people; typical instruments include the accordion (or concertino), rubboard (washboard or frottoir), fiddle, guitar, bass, drums, and sometimes saxophone or other wind instruments

Instruments

auxiliary percussion	Percussion instruments that add color or contrast in an orchestra or band (page 43)
banjo	A folk instrument related to the guitar, with a fretted fingerboard, long neck, a circular body, and four or five strings
bass drum	A large drum with a cylindrical body and two drumheads, both of which can be struck to produce a low, resonant sound
bassoon	A low-pitched woodwind instrument with a double reed
bell	A hollow metal percussion instrument that is sounded by a clapper (hanging or loose) inside or a striker outside
bow	A tool like a long stick made of wood and horsehair that is drawn across the strings of a string instrument to make the sound
brass	The family of wind instruments made of brass and played by buzzing the lips into a mouthpiece
Brazilian percussion	A group of instruments including surdo, agogo bells, cuica, pandeiro, and repinique (page 82)
cello	The tenor voice and second largest member of the string family, whose range falls between that of the viola and the double bass, played by resting the instrument between the knees while seated and plucking or bowing the strings

clarinet	A woodwind instrument having a straight, cylindrical tube with a flaring bell and a single-reed mouthpiece
cymbals	A metal percussion instrument consisting of two round plates held by straps and sounded by striking them together
dàn bâù	A single-string instrument from Vietnam made of wood or bamboo, played by plucking the string and pulling the spout, or wammy bar, forward and back to change the pitch
double bass/string bass	The bass voice and lowest range in the string family, this is the largest string instrument and is often played standing up either by plucking or bowing the strings
double reed	Two joined reeds that vibrate against each other when blown into and form a type of a mouthpiece on some woodwind instruments
drum	A percussion instrument consisting of a hollow shell or cylinder with a drumhead (plastic or skin) stretched over one or both ends that sounds when struck with the hands, sticks, wire brushes, or mallets
electronic organ	A keyboard instrument that was the first musical instrument with electronically generated sound
English horn	A double-reed woodwind instrument similar to but larger than the oboe
fiddle	A name used for the violin when performing folk music
flute	A high-pitched instrument of the woodwind family
French horn	A valved brass wind instrument with a circular shape, tapering from a flaring bell to a narrow mouthpiece
glockenspiel	A melodic percussion instrument with a high range, consisting of thin metal bars (often shiny steel) that sound when struck by mallets
güiro	A percussion instrument made of a dried gourd cut with parallel grooves that produces a scraping sound when a stick is drawn across the grooves
guitar	A plucked or strummed stringed instrument used often by folk and rock musicians, with six or more strings, frets (usually 19), a shape something between a pear and a figure eight, and a round sound hole
hammered dulcimer	A folk instrument with many strings attached to a wooden box and played by striking the strings with little hammers
harpsichord	A keyboard instrument sounded by pressing a key, which activates a plectrum that plucks a string; a keyboard instrument whose strings are plucked (page 120)
Indian percussion	A group of instruments including sitar, sarod, vina, tabla, mridangam, tambura, and badregali (page 81)
jingle bells	A metal percussion instrument consisting of a set of bells fastened together that sound when shaken
keyboard family	A group of instruments including piano, organ, and harpsichord that are sounded by pressing a key (page 120)
koto	A Japanese musical instrument, six feet long, consisting of 13 strings stretched over 13 bridges on an oblong wooden box, and played by three tsume (claws) on the fingers that pluck the strings
mallet percussion	Pitched percussion instruments played by striking with mallets
metal	A category of percussion instruments whose sound is made by the striking together of metal parts
metallophone	A melodic percussion instrument consisting of metal bars attached to a wooden box that sound when struck by mallets
oboe	A slender double-reed woodwind instrument with a conical bore
panpipe	A wind instrument that is played by blowing across the top open ends
percussion	musical instruments in which sound is produced by striking or shaking (page 15)
piano	A keyboard instrument sounded by pressing a key that activates a hammer that strikes a string tuned to a specific pitch (page 120)
piccolo	A small flute pitched an octave above a regular flute

pipa	A Chinese lute (a musical instrument like a guitar) made of wood with bamboo frets, played by plucking the four strings
pipe organ	An instrument with keyboards played by the hands and feet and sounded by pressing down a key or pedal that sends air through wood or metal pipes of many different sizes to create a variety of tone colors and pitches (page 120)
recorder	A woodwind instrument with finger holes played by blowing through a reedless mouthpiece at the top (page 29)
rhythm sticks	A wood percussion instrument that is sounded by scraping or striking one upon the other or on another surface
saxophone	A metal single-reed woodwind instrument in a variety of sizes
sitar	A Middle Eastern string instrument with a long neck, 20 movable frets to produce a wide variety of modes and tunings, and originally having three strings (modern sitars usually have 17 strings), which are plucked to make the sound
skins	A category of percussion instruments whose sound is made by striking (with an implement or the hands) a membrane or piece of plastic that has been stretched over the end of a hollow shell or cylinder
snare drum	A small double-headed drum having wires or cords stretched across the lower head to increase reverberation
steel drums	Mallet percussion instruments made from oil drums or barrels whose tops have been hammered to create various pitches (page 75)
taiko	A large Japanese barrel-shaped drum with a wooden shell and two skin heads that is played with two sticks (page 91)
timpani	A drum with a tunable head and copper bowl, played in sets of two to five
trombone	A brass musical instrument consisting of a long cylindrical tube bent upon itself twice, ending in a bell-shaped mouth, and having a movable U-shaped slide for producing different pitches
trumpet	A brass wind instrument consisting of a long metal tube looped once and ending in a flared bell
tuba	A large brass wind instrument with a very low sounding pitch, played while seated
viola	The alto voice and second-highest pitched member of the string family, lower in pitch than the violin, and higher in pitch than the cello, played by holding the instrument under the chin and either plucking or bowing the strings
violin	The soprano voice and highest-pitched member of the string family, played by holding the instrument under the chin and either plucking or bowing the strings
Welsh harp	A wooden many-string instrument from Wales, usually about six feet tall and in the shape of a triangle, played while sitting and plucking the strings with the fingers
wood	A category of percussion instruments whose sound is made by the striking together of wooden parts
woodblock	A wood percussion instrument whose sound is made by striking a block of wood with a wooden mallet or striker
woodwind	The family of wind instruments whose tubular resonating chambers were originally made of wood and now are sometimes made of plastic; these are played by blowing air across a mouthpiece or reeds, causing the air column in the resonating chamber to vibrate and create the characteristic sound of that instrument
xylophone	A melodic percussion instrument consisting of wooden bars that sound when struck by mallets

Musical Symbols

bar line   A line that goes from the bottom to the top of a staff and divides the staff into measures

bass clef   The clef for lower vocal and instrumental parts (page 115)

breath mark   Used to indicate where a singer or wind instrument player should breathe

clef   A symbol placed at the beginning of a staff to identify the lines and spaces

coda   A short ending section of music (page 108)

crescendo   Gradually becoming louder (page 109)

dal segno (D.S.)   Go back to the ✵ sign and resume singing or playing from there (page 107)

dal segno al coda
D.S. ✵ al Coda   Go back to the ⊕ sign and resume singing or playing from there until you see "To Coda ✵"; then go to the Coda section and continue until the end (page 107)

decrescendo   Gradually becoming softer (page 109)

double bar line   Two bar lines placed at the end of a staff to point out the end of a section or composition

fermata   A symbol that means to hold or pause (all parts), or stretch the sound longer than it normally would be heard or performed

flat ♭   A symbol that lowers the pitch of a note one half step (page 31)

forte *f*   A mark in music that tells musicians to perform at a loud or strong dynamic level (page 52)

grand staff   A set of staves joined together that indicates the joined staves should be performed as one staff (page 114)

line note   A written note with a staff line through its center

piano *p*   A mark in music that tells musicians to perform at a soft or quiet dynamic level (page 47)

mezzo forte *mf*   Medium loud (page 52)

mezzo piano *mp*   Medium soft (page 47)

natural ♮   Neither sharp nor flat; a symbol that cancels an existing sharp or flat, changing the tone by one half step (page 56)

273

pianissimo *pp*		Very soft (page 109)
repeat sign		Two dots in the second and third spaces in front of a double bar line telling you to play or sing the section of music over again from the beginning. A forward repeat sign has two dots after the double bar line and tells you to repeat only from that point on.
sharp ♯		A symbol that raises the pitch of a note one half step (page 31)
slur		A curved line connecting different notes on a staff to indicate they are to be performed smoothly (page 109)
space note		A note written between the lines on a staff
tie		A curved line connecting or tying together two notes of the same pitch indicating they are to be played as if they were one note (page 109)
time signature $\frac{4}{4}$		The symbol at the beginning of the staff that indicates the meter. The upper number indicates the number of beats in each measure, and the lower number indicates which kind of note receives the beat (page 43)
treble clef		The clef for higher vocal and instrumental parts (page 30)

Notation

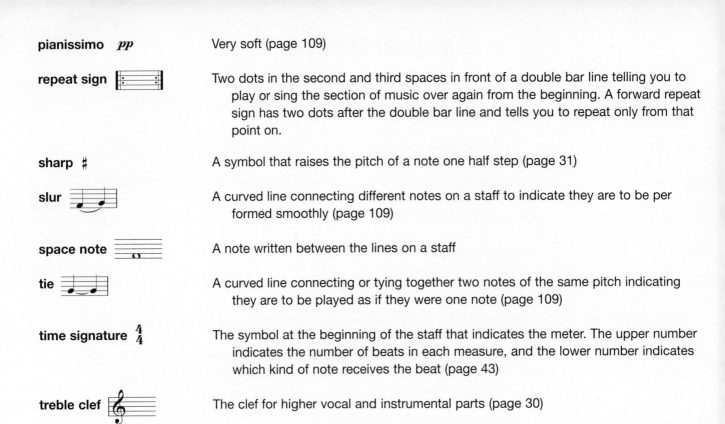

sixteenth notes

eighth notes

eighth quarter dot

quarter note

quarter note dot

quarter dot eighth

quarter rest

half note

half note dot

half rest

whole note

whole rest

syncopa

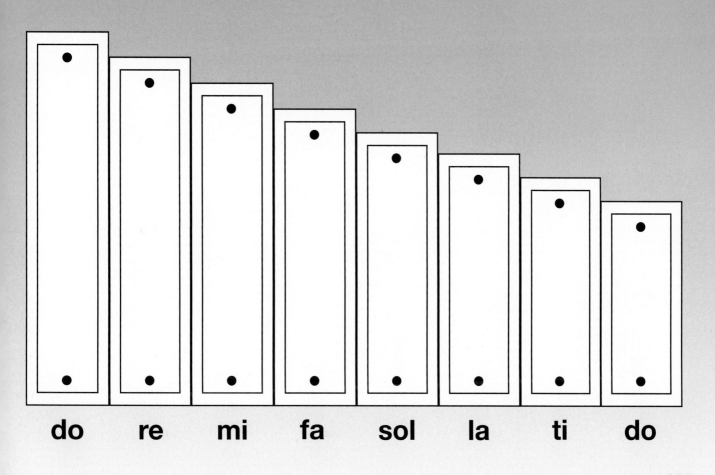

Recorder Fingering Chart

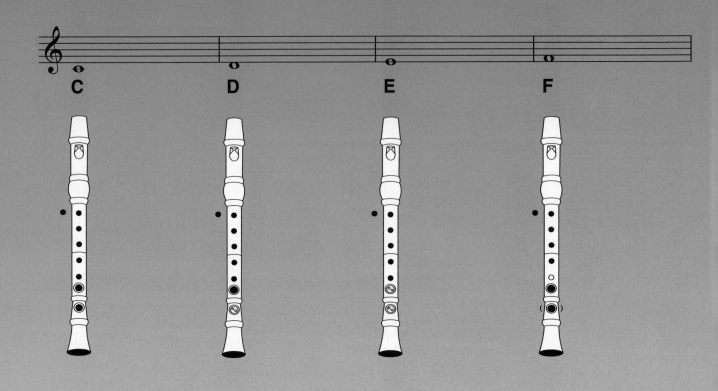

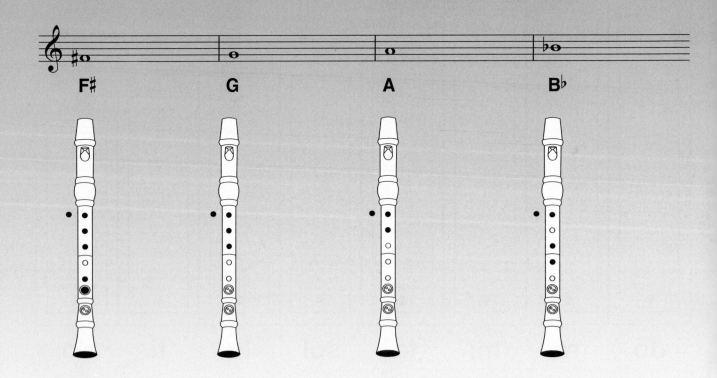

Recorder Fingering Chart

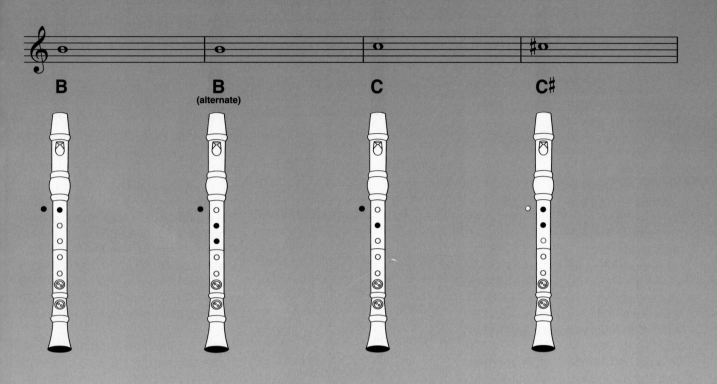

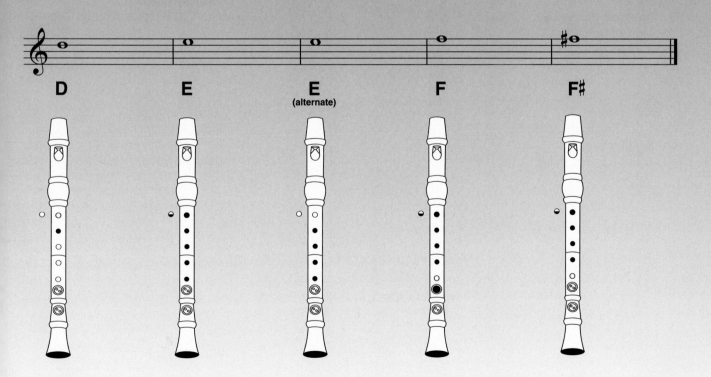

Index

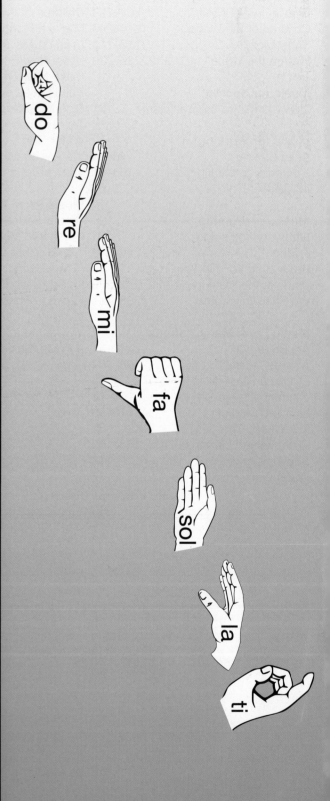